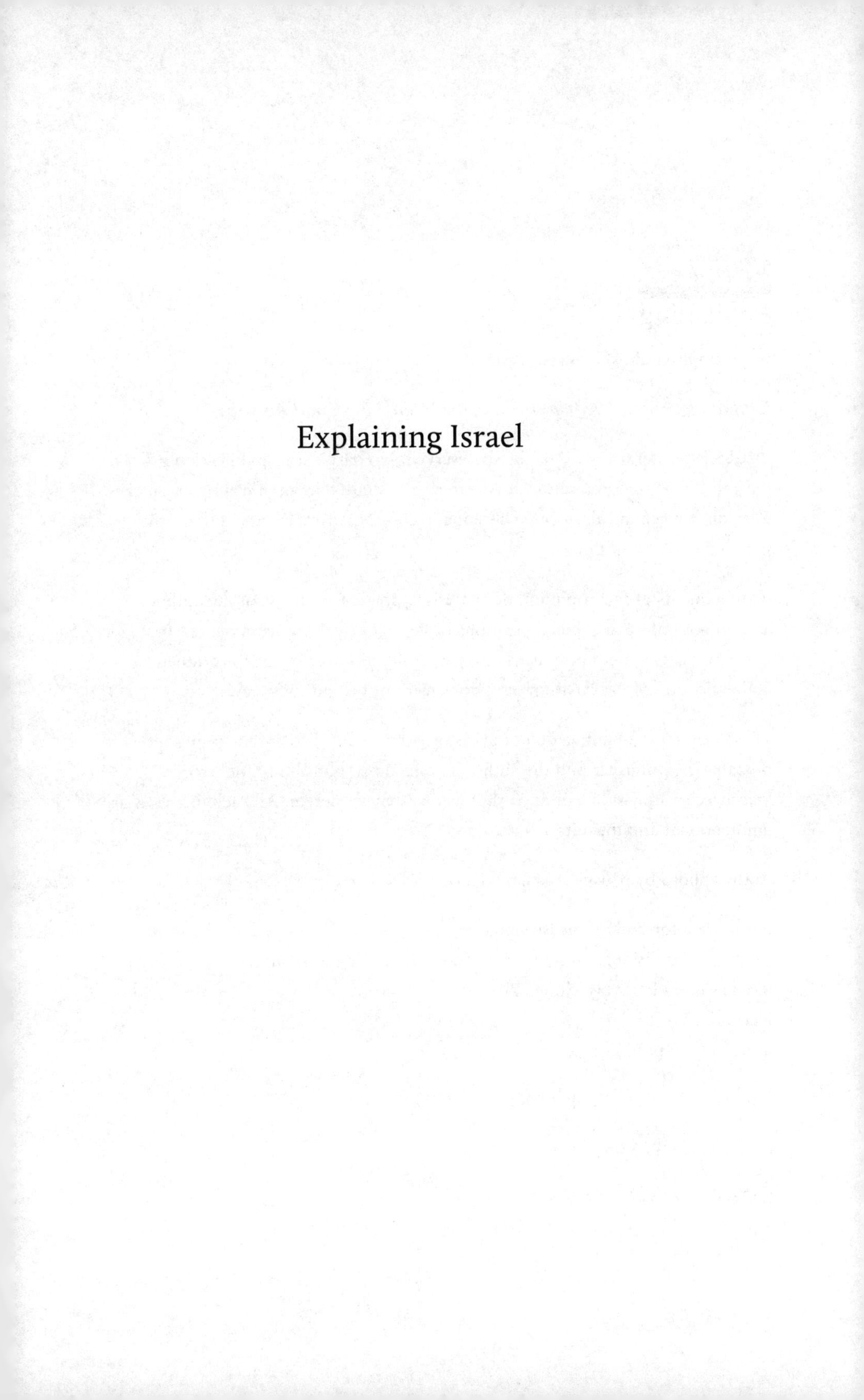

Explaining Israel

www.amplifypublishinggroup.com

Explaining Israel: The Jewish State, the Middle East, and America

Author photo by Moshe Zusman | HeadshotDC.

For more information, please contact:
RealClear Publishing, an imprint of Amplify Publishing Group
620 Herndon Parkway, Suite 220
Herndon, VA 20170
info@amplifypublishing.com

Library of Congress Control Number: 2025904375

CPSIA Code: PRV0525A

ISBN-13: 979-8-89138-375-3

Printed in the United States

Explaining ISRAEL

The Jewish State, the Middle East, and America

PETER BERKOWITZ

RealClear Publishing

CONTENTS

PREFACE

This book collects 40 columns that I published at RealClearPolitics between 2014 and 2024 revolving around Israel, Middle East politics, and American interests in the region. The columns cover an extraordinary period in Israel's history—then again, what decade in the life of the young nation has been anything less than extraordinary?

The essays commence with Israel, the nation-state of the Jewish people and the Middle East's only rights-protecting democracy, at the height of its prosperity and self-confidence. They explore the intensifying schisms inside Israel during years of plenty and the gathering dangers along Israel's borders and throughout the region. They delve into the searing controversy over constitutional essentials provoked in January 2023 by Prime Minister Benjamin Netanyahu's government's sweeping proposals for judicial reform. They grapple with the October 7, 2023, massacre perpetrated by Iran-backed Hamas jihadists, follow Israelis' remarkable resilience through horror and heartbreak, and examine the multifront war—as 2024 draws to a close, no end is in sight—into which Iran and its regional proxies plunged the Jewish state.

The essays also highlight the convergence of two American interests. One, dating to the onset of the Cold War, is in a stable Middle East that favors freedom. The other is America's interest in a free and democratic Israel capable of defending itself in a neighborhood rife with authoritarian nationalism and Islamic extremism.

I wrote several of the essays during, and all have been colored by, regular visits to Israel. On those trips I encountered the many sides of the Israeli spirit and witnessed up close the complexity of the Jewish state.

The essays occasionally quote but constantly draw on conversations with a fascinating mix of characters, from good friends to strangers, belonging to the great Israeli mosaic: left, center, and right; secular, traditional, modern Orthodox, and ultra-Orthodox Jews; Muslim, Christian, and Druze citizens; residents of Tel Aviv, Jerusalem, Judea and Samaria, Haifa, the Galilee, the Golan Heights, the Negev, and Eilat; West Bank Palestinian scholars, political leaders, and refugee camp residents; Israel Defense Forces soldiers and officers (both regular and reserve), retired commanders, and former high-ranking officials in the intelligence and internal security services; think tank scholars and NGO staff and leadership; politicians and bureaucrats; contractors and winemakers; grade school and high school students and teachers, university students and professors, yeshiva students and rabbis; artists, dancers, musicians, actors, and directors; waiters, waitresses, chefs, and restaurateurs; lawyers, doctors, and business executives; print and broadcast journalists, novelists, and publishers; tour guides and bartenders; kiosk workers, small-business owners, high-tech entrepreneurs, and international investors; cab drivers, bus drivers, yoga instructors, therapists, and kibbutzniks; and more.

The essays appear in this volume for the most part as RealClearPolitics originally published them. Here and there I have added or edited lightly for the purposes of clarification. Links in the originals have either been changed to footnotes or dropped. With the benefit of hindsight, and leavened by persistent study and steady accumulation of experience in the region and in Washington, I would today phrase matters more precisely, structure arguments more elegantly, and present evidence more tellingly. But a valuable part of the historical record consists of how observers described unfolding events and emerging ideas.

Professors continue to debate whether events or ideas take precedence in the study of politics. Since it is not necessary to pick a winner to recognize that both are essential, the columns gathered here weave together the news of events with what the late *Wall Street Journal* editorial page editor Robert Bartley called "the news of ideas." Accordingly, the columns regularly report insights from, and take issue with, articles and books that address the dilemmas of Israeli politics and the conduct and objectives of US foreign policy.

The inevitable repetition in a collection of columns has its advantages—underscoring continuities, illuminating turning points, and bringing into focus related but distinct issues. Repetition is bound to be more pronounced where pieces situate pressing public-policy debates, major partisan clashes, and abiding national security threats in the broader political and geopolitical context.

Time and again, the columns collected here stress Israel's founding commitment: the establishment of the nation-state of the Jewish people in their ancestral homeland as a rights-protecting democracy. And they frequently highlight not only America's interest in ensuring that Israel has the means to defend itself on the battlefield, but also America's interest in taking the side of the Middle East's only liberal democracy in the corridors of power, including in the assembly rooms and chambers of international organizations, against the authoritarianism and barbarism that menace the region.

More than half of the essays deal with two crises that struck Israel in the last two years. The government's determination to carry out a fundamental overhaul of the judiciary rocked the Jewish state between

January 4, 2023, and October 6, 2023, igniting years of pent-up bitterness and distrust. The jihadist savagery—the slaughter of civilians, the use of rape as a weapon of war, and the kidnapping of children, teenagers, adults, and the elderly—unleashed by Hamas on Israel's southern communities on October 7, 2023, let loose a wave of fear, grief, fury, and bewilderment that swept the country and inflicted traumas that will forever shape the nation.

As they sought to regain their bearings, free the hostages, and destroy Hamas's capacity to wage war and govern Gaza, Israelis were dismayed to hear accusations from abroad that by exercising its right of self-defense against those pledged to its destruction Israel was committing genocide. And Israelis observed with incredulity and trepidation the large pro-jihadist rallies in European streets and the numerous anti-Israel encampments on American university campuses. To many Israelis, it seemed that the civilized world had turned upside down.

Fear for Israel's future runs deep among its citizens. So, too, does courage in the face of monstrous evil and steadfastness in pursuit of the Zionist dream. Israelis have much to be proud of and much with which to contend. Both the Jewish state's breathtaking achievements and its formidable challenges are crucial to explaining Israel.

Several individuals and organizations made indispensable contributions to this book. RealClearPolitics Executive Editor Carl Cannon did his best to tame my wordiness while providing a choice forum for explaining Israel to American readers. Week in, week out, RealClearPolitics copyeditors Tom Kavanagh, Cathi Warren, and Anne Welty brought my prose into conformity with the imperatives of AP style and sound English while graciously accommodating last-minute changes. The Hoover Institution at Stanford University has served as my home base for nearly two decades. Under directors John Raisian, Tom Gilligan, and Condoleezza Rice, and with the long-standing financial backing of Tad and Dianne Taube, Hoover has given me wide latitude to pursue and has steadily supported research and writing on a variety of matters connected to freedom and democracy at home and abroad, not least Israel, Middle East politics, and America.

My Hoover research associate Emily "Sleevs" Messner improved every essay in this book with her sharp eye for, and low tolerance of, ambiguous wording, imprecise arguments, inconclusive or inapt evidence, and tendentious formulations. Jacob Leon thoughtfully proofread the page proofs. At regular lunches, my friend Stanley Kurtz asked hard questions and offered incisive observations, not least that my original working title was terrible. The Paul E. Singer Foundation, a stalwart champion of American constitutional government and of Israel as the free and democratic nation-state of the Jewish people, provided a generous grant to facilitate publication.

Peter Berkowitz
Washington, DC
December 2024

INTRODUCTION

In 2014 Israel's future had never seemed brighter. Led by the high-tech sector, the economy was booming. The Israel Defense Forces—with advanced weapons, an outstanding air force, sophisticated intelligence capabilities, and cybersecurity prowess—gave the Jewish state the most powerful military in the Middle East. While not producing warm relations and bustling commerce, treaties with Egypt (1979) and Jordan (1994) brought cold peace and stability along Israel's two longest land borders. World surveys placed Israelis among the happiest of populations. In a country whose national security interests compelled it to impose mandatory military service on men and women, life expectancy ranked among the longest in the West. Secular Israeli women had higher fertility rates than secular women in any country in the West; those of their ultra-Orthodox sisters were significantly higher. Israel pumped plentiful amounts of natural gas from offshore fields that had come online during the previous decade. Over the previous 30 years, the country had gone from a few vineyards making largely cheap wine for sacramental purposes to around 300 vineyards producing a variety of fine wines. And with its bustling commerce, stunning Mediterranean beachfront, culinary delights, thriving culture, and work-hard-play-hard spirit, Tel Aviv had become one of the world's most exciting, and expensive, cities.

At the same time, and generally ignored or downplayed by much of the population and more than a few political leaders, Israel's enemies strengthened their capabilities and plotted the Jewish state's demise. In the summer of 2014, Iran-backed Hamas jihadists kidnapped and brutally murdered three young Israeli men in Judea and Samaria—the biblical names, used with increasing regularity in Israel, for the West Bank. Subsequently, Iran-backed Hamas jihadists in Gaza showered southern Israeli communities with rockets. In response, Israel conducted a seven-week military campaign in Gaza, Operation Protective Edge, to degrade Hamas's ability to launch rockets at Israel's civilian population, but not to destroy the organization or remove it from power. In Lebanon to the north, Iran-backed Hezbollah had amassed a vast arsenal of projectiles aimed at Israel—by that time tens of thousands of ordinary rockets, precision-guided rockets, and intermediate-range missiles—while its fighters gained battlefield experience in the Syrian civil war. The Islamic Republic of Iran made steady progress toward constructing nuclear weapons; insulating its nuclear program from attack; producing ballistic missiles; and funding, training, and equipping not only Hamas and Hezbollah on Israel's borders but also other militias around the region.

As external threats intensified in 2014 and in the following years, internal strife in Israel mounted. Members of the working class, often Mizrahi Jews with roots in the Muslim-majority countries of North Africa and the Middle East, resented the well-educated, highly remunerated, and progressive Israeli elites, in large measure Ashkenazi Jews hailing from families that had emigrated from, or could trace their ancestry to, Europe. While priding themselves on their commitment to equality and pluralism, Israel's Ashkenazi elites often looked down on Mizrahi Jews' traditional beliefs and practices. Meanwhile, much of the non-ultra-Orthodox majority angrily objected to the ultra-Orthodox minority's exemption from military service and to the substantial subsidies that the government allocated to their religious schools (in 2014 the ultra-Orthodox constituted about 11 percent of the population and by 2024 about 13.5 percent). Although Israel had made considerable progress in improving the social and economic wellbeing of its Arab minority—around 21 percent of the citizenry—much remained to be done.

Internal strife over the status and future of West Bank Palestinians in 2014 was muted, but the dilemma for the Jewish state persisted. In the 1967 Six-Day War, Israel seized the West Bank—including the old city of Jerusalem and the heartland of biblical Israel—from Jordan and the Gaza Strip from Egypt (as well as the Golan Heights, home to Druze communities but no Palestinian ones, from Syria). In 2005 Israel evacuated every Israeli soldier and civilian from Gaza; in short order Hamas ousted the Palestinian Authority (PA) and seized control. But approximately 3 million West Bank Palestinians, notwithstanding exercising considerable autonomy in civil and political matters, continue to live under Israeli military rule in Judea and Samaria.

It is reasonable to maintain—contrary to the dominant opinion among diplomats, professors, and journalists—that Israel does not occupy the West Bank because the territory had never been widely recognized as part of a sovereign nation-state (Jordan's 1950 annexation of the West Bank was only recognized by three countries), at least not since the fall of the second Jewish commonwealth in AD 70. Yet the legal issue obscures the overarching political dilemma. Over the long run, Israel cannot remain a rights-protecting democracy while ruling over a population to which it declines to grant citizenship, and it cannot remain a Jewish state if it grants citizenship to millions more non-Jews. Nevertheless, if Israel were to withdraw from Judea and Samaria, then, as in Gaza, Hamas would overthrow the PA, and the jihadists would impose a second Iran-backed Islamist theocracy pledged to Israel's destruction on the nation's border—this one overlooking Israel's cultural, commercial, and population center.

From 2014 to 2018, their churning economy and the relative quiet on their borders distracted Israelis from the troubling developments from without and from within. Many, not least in the political establishment, supposed that Israeli deterrence operated effectively. The state-of the-art Iron Dome defense system intercepted most of Hamas's occasional rocket fire. Hezbollah had not disrupted life in Israel since the end of the 2006 Second Lebanon War. Prime Minister Benjamin Netanyahu, who had led Israel since 2009, assured the public that he was the man to prevent Iran from acquiring nuclear weapons.

The new affluence also diverted people's attention from the erosion under Netanyahu's watch of Israeli political cohesion—the sense among citizens that their remarkably diverse population formed one people devoted to a common national enterprise. Enmities—between ordinary citizens and the elites, the secular and the religious, Netanyahu's voters and the opposition—steadily worsened, in no small measure owing to the state attorney's investigation of Netanyahu for bribery, fraud, and breach of trust. Launched in 2016, the investigation produced an indictment in November 2019 and proceeded in May 2020 to a trial that, more than four years later, has reached no resolution. Netanyahu's camp views the investigation, the indictment, and the trial as stemming from charges fabricated by a desperate political establishment that could not defeat him at the polls. Led by Netanyahu, they have portrayed the opposition as an enemy within.

A sharply split nation, Israel conducted five closely contested elections between April 2019 and November 2022. Netanyahu maintained control following each of the first three. The fourth election brought to power an unlikely governing coalition, headed by conservative Naftali Bennett and centrist Yair Lapid—each took a turn as prime minister—that included eight parties spanning the right, center, and left and, for the first time in 50 years, an Arab-Israeli party. With the fifth election in three and a half years, Netanyahu, by then Israel's longest-serving prime minister and on trial, returned to power, scraping through by a mere 30,000 votes out of approximately 4.8 million cast. The intensity of the opposition's hostility toward Netanyahu, from center-right to left, gave him only one option for forming a government. Half of his coalition consisted of two extreme elements of Israeli politics: the ultra-Orthodox, who not only enjoy an exemption from military service but whose adult male population also often shun the labor force in favor of full-time, state-subsidized religious study; and religious ultranationalists, who prioritize retaining Israeli control over Judea and Samaria.

Two major crises have defined Netanyahu's sixth government, which took office on December 29, 2022. The first, a self-inflicted wound, erupted less than a week later. Although Netanyahu had not made it a campaign issue, on January 4, 2023, Justice Minister Yariv Levin announced a far-reaching judicial overhaul. While Israel's exceptionally progressive and activist Supreme Court needed substantial reform, the government's poorly rolled out and ill-considered proposals, if adopted, would have undermined the independence of Israel's judiciary.

The proposals sparked massive protests week after week throughout the country, shook investors' confidence in the nation's political stability, and impelled reservists, not least air force pilots, to threaten to decline to report for training on the grounds that the government sought to destroy Israel's democratic character. In response, the government accused the opposition of fomenting anarchy and undermining military readiness. The controversy eroded morale, damaged the economy, and drove Israel to the brink of constitutional crisis.

That constitutional crisis was averted on October 7 by a terrifying national security crisis. Israelis responded swiftly, bravely, and resolutely to the massacre perpetrated by thousands of Hamas jihadists on the day Israelis refer to as "the black Sabbath." Over the next few days, hundreds of thousands of reservists dropped everything to join their units and defend their country against Islamist terrorists whose battle plan, in manifest violation of the laws of war, called for fighting in civilian clothes; killing, raping, and kidnapping Israeli civilians; turning Palestinians into human shields by operating from within and under Gaza's civilian areas; and using Palestinians as human sacrifices, counting on their corpses to win sympathy for Hamas's cause.

Even as international institutions geared up to condemn Israel's exercise of its right to self-defense, and American university students and professors organized demonstrations in support of Hamas terrorists, Israeli soldiers and officers adopted rules of engagement that respected the international laws of war. Israelis from all walks of life prepared meals for the troops around the clock at Tel Aviv restaurants and delivered them to the front lines. Parents of soldiers led efforts that raised millions of dollars to purchase essential military equipment. Retirees picked fruits and vegetables in untended fields. Combat veterans organized to provide counseling and schooling for the displaced and the bereaved. These, along with countless more acts of quiet valor, exhibited the vibrant and resilient spirit of Israeli society.

This spirit blends the free, the democratic, and the Jewish principles of the nation-state proclaimed in Israel's 1948 Declaration of Independence. It energizes and elevates the individuals and communities responsible for Israel's splendid achievements. And it fortifies the Jewish state to meet its formidable challenges.

1

BUILD THE INFRASTRUCTURE FOR ARAB-ISRAELI PEACE

March 17, 2014

TEL AVIV—A perception has increasingly taken hold that the threat to Israel from conventional military operations has never been slighter. This assessment has prompted some on the left, here and in the United States, to conclude that Israel should make significant concessions in US-led negotiations with the Palestinians.

Both the assessment and the conclusion are flawed and dangerous.

While Israel should advance its interests by taking well-calibrated steps to ease the conflict with the Palestinians, it must do so with clear eyes on the serious security threats, new as well as old, that the Jewish state confronts.

These threats stem from the volatility that marks the Middle East. Fundamental instability has defined the region since well before the Jewish state's birth in 1948, amid a war launched by its Arab neighbors to destroy it. And fundamental instability is likely to persist.

No Arab army today has the *intention* of invading Israel. But the Egyptian Army, Jordanian Army, Syrian Army, and the army of Iran-backed

Hezbollah, which constitutes a state within a state in southern Lebanon, maintain formidable arsenals with the *capacity* to inflict punishing blows.

It is true that the Israeli Air Force, with the aid of Israeli intelligence, operates with impunity in its neighborhood, as it showed by destroying Syria's nuclear reactor in 2007 and launching six air strikes last year on Iran-supplied weapons en route from Syria to Hezbollah. Earlier this month Israeli navy commandos, with the aid of Israeli intelligence, demonstrated their mettle by seizing in the Red Sea a ship from Iran carrying weapons—bullets, mortars, and rockets—intended for Gaza.

Nevertheless, Israel faces no shortage of additional dangers.

While the Palestinians cannot defeat Israel militarily, the Palestinian Authority refuses to recognize Israel as a Jewish state. This refusal, which is entwined with aggressive PA-sponsored incitement of hatred against Israel and the persistent claim that some 5 million Palestinians around the world possess the right to take up residence within Israel's pre-1967 borders, prolongs a conflict that saps the Israeli spirit and drains precious material and financial resources.

Moreover, between Iran-backed Hamas to the south in the Gaza Strip and Hezbollah to the north, 70,000 rockets and missiles target Israel, a significant portion of which can reach Tel Aviv. Most perilous is Iran's quest for regional hegemony through the export of terror and the acquisition of nuclear weapons, which threatens to unleash a nuclear arms race among Middle Eastern states and heightens the chilling prospect of a nuclear device falling into jihadists' hands.

Shock waves emanating from the uprisings in the Arab world in 2011 exacerbate these dangers. Disarray of varying kinds has impaired the ability of the states on Israel's borders (Egypt, Jordan, Syria, and Lebanon) to control their territories. The threat of regime collapse all around reinforces the Netanyahu government's core conviction: A viable resolution of the conflict with the Palestinians—preferably a peace treaty that creates a demilitarized Palestinian state that recognizes Israel as the nation-state of the Jewish people and brings an end to hostilities and all claims—must leave Israel with secure borders and the ability to defend itself against new iterations of the fundamental instability the region has long known.

Consider the following:

To the southwest, Egypt, the largest Arab state with a population of 82.5 million, is in effect governed by the military. Led by Field Marshal Abdel Fattah al-Sisi, the Egyptian army took control of Egypt in a July 2012 military coup, replacing Muslim Brotherhood leader Mohamed Morsi's authoritarian regime, which in June 2012 was democratically elected to succeed President Hosni Mubarak's authoritarian regime, which fell in February 2011. Since then, an already fragile Egyptian economy has suffered sharp declines in tourism and foreign investment. Feeding the population presents a major challenge. Meanwhile, Egypt's Sinai Peninsula has become a lawless region, a haven for smugglers of merchandise and weapons, traffickers in drugs and human beings, and jihadists of various sects, including al-Qaeda.

On Israel's northeastern border, Syria, wracked by a three-year civil war, has become a magnet and training ground for jihadists from around the globe. President Bashar al-Assad, backed by predominantly Shia Iran, rules about 40 percent of the country. A sizable proportion of rebels are Sunni jihadists fighting to create an Islamic state. The death toll in Syria's civil war is approaching 150,000, far more than all the Arab deaths in almost a century of violence marking the Arab-Israeli conflict. Despite, or because of, a Russian-brokered September 2013 deal, Assad remains in possession of much of his chemical weapons arsenal. And Syria exports instability: According to the UN Refugee Agency (UNHCR), in addition to 6.5 million internally displaced Syrians, the civil war has produced 2.5 million refugees, and by year's end, the number could swell to 4 million.[1]

---

1 "Remarks by António Guterres, United Nations High Commissioner for Refugees," OSCE Permanent Council, February 20, 2014, https://www.osce.org/pc/111523.

About a million Syrian refugees have flooded into Lebanon, representing nearly 20 percent of the tiny nation's population. Predominantly Sunni, the refugees have dramatically tilted Lebanon's delicate balance among Sunnis, Shias, and Christians, substantially increasing the explosiveness of an explosive situation. Meanwhile, Shia Hezbollah fighters in Syria supporting Assad are gaining valuable battlefield experience. And despite Israel's noteworthy interventions—the efforts of the United Nations Interim Force in Lebanon, whose job it is to prevent Hezbollah in southern Lebanon from rearming, have been negligible—Hezbollah is acquiring in Syria sophisticated weapons for the next round of hostilities with Israel.

The UNHCR estimates that Jordan, which has absorbed approximately 600,000 Syrian refugees, will take in another 200,000 by the end of 2014. This puts huge pressure on services and resources in the fragile pro-Western monarchy of about 8 million, home to a majority Palestinian population and a significant Muslim Brotherhood opposition. Israeli experts mordantly joke that Jordan has been tottering for 70 years now, but few competent observers here doubt that King Abdullah II faces formidable challenges. His fall would likely turn Israel's quiet eastern border into another haven for jihadists and one more launching pad for rockets and missiles aimed at Israel's civilian population.

Over the last decade, a fractious Arab world intermittently united by opposition to Israel has been supplanted by a fractious Arab world increasingly divided by Sunni-Shia conflict. The toppling of Saddam Hussein in 2003 by an American-led coalition had the unintended consequence of reigniting a struggle that dates to the seventh-century schism in Islam over Muhammad's successor. Iran's quest to establish a Shia crescent stretching from the eastern side of the Persian Gulf through Iraq to Syria and Lebanon and their Mediterranean ports has fanned the flames of the Sunni-Shia struggle. The Arab upheavals of 2011 made the struggle the region's central dynamic.

Such instability makes even more necessary, and more difficult, Israel's separation from the Palestinians—a separation that Prime Minister Ariel Sharon set in motion in 2005 by disengaging from Gaza and removing every Israeli civilian and soldier from the territory.

The separation is necessary because the free and democratic conscience with which a substantial majority of Israelis are endowed will not permit them to rule over another people in perpetuity. It is also necessary because the commitment to a Jewish state among a substantial majority of Israelis cannot be reconciled with the absorption of millions of Palestinians into Israel. And it is necessary because the longer Israel rules another people, even if compelled by security considerations, the greater the strain on its Jewish conscience.

The separation is difficult because Palestinians appear unwilling to agree to diplomatic conditions and security measures that Israel deems essential. Not least is Palestinian recognition of Israel as a Jewish state. This, the Netanyahu government believes, would amount to a formal declaration by the Palestinians of the end of claims against Israel, and it is no mere formality. It would signal the PA's readiness to cease incitement and would constitute Palestinian renunciation of the alleged right of generations of descendants of the original Palestinian refugees to live within Israel's pre-1967 borders.

Israel cannot compel the Palestinians to reach a reasonable and comprehensive agreement on borders, security, refugees, and Jerusalem. But in the increasingly likely event that Secretary of State John Kerry's efforts fail to bear fruit, Israel should encourage the United States to take alternative steps to advance resolution of the conflict.

Foremost among these, the United States should lead wealthy Gulf Arab states, the EU, supportive members of the international community, and Palestinians themselves in raising money for institution building in the West Bank. Israel should vigorously cooperate behind the scenes. The initiative should focus on creating the infrastructure—physical, economic, educational, political, and cultural—of a future Palestinian state. This would heighten the likelihood of the state's success as soon as political circumstances permit its birth.

Focusing on building infrastructure for a future Palestinian state could seem a tepid next step. But in a region marked by fundamental instability, it may represent the best option—one that eases the friction between Israel and Palestinians and contributes to the construction of a more stable Middle East.

2

A ONE-STATE MIDEAST SOLUTION? IT WON'T WORK

April 3, 2014, discussing The Israeli Solution: A One-State Plan for Peace in the Middle East *by Caroline Glick*

In the two decades since President Bill Clinton watched Israeli Prime Minister Yitzhak Rabin and Palestine Liberation Organization Chairman Yasser Arafat sign the Oslo Accords on the White House lawn, widespread agreement has emerged about the shape of a just solution to the Israeli-Palestinian conflict. The broad consensus is that Israel should agree to a Palestinian state on lands Israel seized in the 1967 Six-Day War and that Palestinians should not only recognize Israel as the nation-state of the Jewish people but also agree to a secure Israel with defensible borders and terminate all other claims against the Jewish state.

In his final months in office, Clinton tacitly put the prestige of the United States behind such a blueprint. In a June 2002 speech, President George W. Bush did so formally, outlining his Roadmap for Peace, which called for a two-state solution. This followed on the heels of a March 2002 Arab League meeting in Beirut, where Saudi Arabia's Crown Prince Abdullah announced the Arab Peace Initiative, which also endorsed a two-state solution. And in 2009 at Bar-Ilan University, Benjamin

Netanyahu became Israel's first conservative prime minister to declare support for a two-state solution.

Sharp disagreement persists about the contours of a resolution of the conflict, including differences over borders, security arrangements, Palestinian refugees, Israeli settlements, and the status of Jerusalem. That's why many are skeptical that Secretary of State John Kerry will succeed in his quest for a lasting agreement that ends the conflict.

Nevertheless, according to a December 2013 joint Israeli-Palestinian poll, 63 percent of Israelis and 53 percent of Palestinians support the idea of two separate nations coexisting in side-by-side states.

But nothing is ever easy in the Middle East, not even reconciling the results of public opinion polling. A recent survey by Zogby Research Services reported that only about one-third of Israelis and Palestinians currently see a two-nation solution as feasible.

A new book by Caroline Glick, a veteran Middle East observer, fleshes out the reasons for such skepticism. Glick maintains that the establishment of a Palestinian state existing side by side with Israel is "among the most irrational, unsuccessful policies the United States has ever adopted." In *The Israeli Solution: A One-State Plan for Peace in the Middle East*, the prolific and pungent *Jerusalem Post* columnist declares that the two-state solution has "no basis in reality" and "no chance of ever succeeding."

An American-born Israeli who participated as an Israel Defense Forces officer in negotiations with the Palestinians in the mid-1990s and who was an embedded journalist with American troops during the 2003 Iraq invasion, Glick is a hardheaded and intrepid analyst of the region. For more than a decade, she has exposed the sentimentality, sanctimoniousness, and wishful thinking exhibited by would-be peacemakers in Israel and the United States.

Her book puts forward an alternative peace plan. Glick's one-state solution assumes that Israel's disengagement from Gaza is permanent while envisaging "the application of Israeli law—and through it Israeli sovereignty—over the West Bank of the Jordan River." She argues that this is "a viable, realistic option" that is "fair, liberal, and democratic" and would "significantly strengthen Israel's strategic, diplomatic, democratic, demographic, and legal positions."

Her proposal is not only unrealistic; it would also weaken Israel and pose a grave threat to Israel's liberal, democratic, and Jewish character. By inadvertently illuminating the disadvantages of a one-state solution, Glick confirms the wisdom, despite its defects, of a two-state approach.

Glick is right about many matters, particularly the flawed understanding that impairs the analysis of the Israeli-Palestinian conflict by American and European diplomats—and not a few Israeli politicians, pundits, and professors.

For example:

- Much support for the two-state solution is fueled by the mistaken assumption that the absence of a Palestinian state is the root cause of the Arab world's and Iran's hostility toward Israel and of instability throughout the region.
- Many two-state solution proponents, including President Obama, wrongly regard Israeli settlements as the major obstacle to peace while downplaying Palestinian terrorism and the culture that fosters it and overlooking Palestinian Authority corruption and authoritarianism.
- Because the land promised to the Jewish people under the auspices of the League of Nations by the post–World War I British Mandate for Palestine included the West Bank, and because no nation, including Jordan (which controlled the territories between 1949 and 1967), has a superior legal claim, Israel has a respectable case under international law to exercise sovereignty over the West Bank or, to use the biblical names Glick prefers, Judea and Samaria.
- Israel's 1967 seizure of the West Bank was followed by decades of Palestinian gains in economics, civil rights,

> literacy, higher education, and health, while the Arab citizens of Israel, because they possess the same civil and political rights as Jewish Israelis, enjoy greater freedom than any other Arabs in the Middle East.

A one-state solution, however, does not follow from these hard truths.

Glick's argument contains three key elements: Israel has a right to exercise sovereignty of the West Bank, holding the West Bank is critical for Israel's national security, and the approximately 2.2 million West Bank Palestinians will benefit from Israeli rule. The argument doesn't withstand scrutiny.

First, even if Israel could establish its claim to title over Judea and Samaria based on international law and the Jewish people's historic attachment to the heartland of the first Jewish commonwealth thousands of years ago, it would not make it prudent to act on the claim.

Second, Glick contends Israel must hold on to the West Bank to maintain defensible borders. But she ignores the legion of high-ranking IDF officers and civilian experts who believe Israel's security needs could be met by the combination of a demilitarized Palestinian state, Israeli control of the Jordan River Valley, and high-tech surveillance installations strategically located on the high points of the mountain ridge that forms the spine of Judea and Samaria.

Third, she blithely suggests that West Bank Palestinians will prefer Israeli rule because it will provide civil rights and economic opportunities they lack under the PA. She backs up this dubious suggestion with polling of Palestinians that she contends indicate that a majority opposes Israeli withdrawal from the West Bank. But the 2012 poll she cites merely indicates that a majority opposes a particular version of the two-state solution, a part of which involves withdrawal. The survey provides no evidence that West Bank Palestinians would prefer living in the Jewish state. There's ample evidence, moreover, that this very concept is a nonstarter among the Palestinian political leadership and among the Palestinian people.

Another poll she cites, conducted by Ariel University researchers in 2013, finds that "59 percent of Israeli Jews believe that Israel should apply its laws to all or parts of Judea and Samaria." But this hardly means that a majority of Israelis affirm "the sovereign rights of the Jewish people to Judea and Samaria." The finding is compatible with a majority believing that Israeli law should be applied only to the major settlement blocs—between 3 and 10 percent of the West Bank—within the framework of a two-state solution.

Glick's poll-driven arguments appear half-hearted. Her real view, stated robustly and repeatedly, seems to be that the Palestinians, and Arabs more generally, are resolutely opposed to living in peace and harmony with Israel. That assessment, however, cannot be reconciled with a single free, democratic, Jewish, and secure Israel that absorbs West Bank Palestinians.

Glick ridicules the idea that "Palestinians and the wider Islamic world" are "by their nature moderate and peaceful." She mocks George W. Bush's conviction that elections would bring democracy to Arab countries. She scoffs at President Obama for supposing "that empowering Islamists was the answer to the region's ills."

Glick argues, moreover, that despite Israel's peace treaties with Egypt and Jordan, "the people of Egypt and Jordan never made peace with Israel." She emphasizes that "hatred of Jews in these and in every other Arab state is endemic, reaching levels of between 98 and 100 percent." And she insists that "Palestinians from every part of the political spectrum have made clear through word and deed that they are uninterested in peacefully coexisting with the Jewish state under any conditions that would allow the Jewish state to survive."

If Glick is right that the root cause of the conflict is Palestinian rejection of Israel's right to exist as a Jewish state, then under her one-state solution, West Bank Palestinians, who would constitute approximately 20 percent of Israel's population—along with today's Arab citizens of Israel, they would constitute around 40 percent of the population—might well refuse

Israeli citizenship and the associated right to vote. This would transform the ugly slander that Israel is an apartheid state into an ugly reality.

Alternatively, Palestinians will demand citizenship, the better to make good on their oft-expressed ambition to create a single non-Jewish state between the Jordan River and the Mediterranean Sea.

Caroline Glick vividly demonstrates that a two-state solution will not bring peace to the greater Middle East and will not dispose of Israel's need for constant vigilance. Yet the baleful scenarios that flow from her one-state solution support the broad consensus in favor of a long-term pursuit of two states for two peoples by vindicating the judgment that it is the least-bad option Israel confronts.

3

NINE QUESTIONS OBAMA WASN'T ASKED ON ISRAEL

June 11, 2015

TEL AVIV—Last week journalist Ilana Dayan interviewed President Obama on her popular Israeli prime-time television program. This was the latest in the president's campaign to take his case for a nuclear agreement with Iran and against Israeli Prime Minister Benjamin Netanyahu directly to the people, particularly the Jewish people. The president launched the campaign in late May in an interview with the *Atlantic*'s Jeffrey Goldberg and followed it with a speech a few days later at Congregation Adas Israel in Washington.

Goldberg and Dayan elicited clarifying answers from the president. Most clarifying were Obama's questionable judgments and policies.

Goldberg and Dayan are accomplished reporters, but extracting a complete account from a sitting president is not easy. To carry forward the task they began, here are nine follow-up questions that would provide information crucial to a more well-rounded assessment of US Middle East policy under the current administration:

1. In his interview with Goldberg, Obama said, "There has been no indication from the Saudis or any other [Gulf Cooperation Council] countries that they have an intention to pursue their own nuclear program."[1] Yet in the *Wall Street Journal* in November 2013, Saudi Prince Alwaleed bin Talal, a prominent member of the Saudi royal family and the Arab world's richest businessman, expressed dismay at the Obama administration's proposed deal with Tehran because it did not require Iran to dismantle its nuclear program. The prince also suggested the possibility, if a bad deal were signed, of the Arabian Peninsula going nuclear. Moreover, only last month the *Journal* quoted a former Saudi official, a retired Saudi colonel, and a Saudi prince and think tank scholar, all of whom agreed that Iran's acquisition of a nuclear weapon would compel Saudi Arabia to obtain one.[2] In a country where an extended ruling family and a small elite keep a tight grip on the reins of power, do these assertions by eminent Saudis, published in a premier American newspaper, not count as significant indications of Saudi and GCC intent?
2. Obama told Goldberg, "Part of the reason why [the GCC countries] would not pursue their own nuclear program—assuming that we have been successful in preventing Iran from continuing down the path of obtaining a nuclear weapon—is that the protection that we provide as their partner is a far greater deterrent than they could ever hope

---

1 Jeffrey Goldberg, "'Look … It's My Name on This': Obama Defends the Iran Nuclear Deal," *Atlantic,* May 21, 2015, https://www.theatlantic.com/international/archive/2015/05/obama-interview-iran-isis-israel/393782.

2 Yaroslav Trofimov, "Saudi Arabia Considers Nuclear Weapons to Offset Iran," *Wall Street Journal,* May 7, 2015, https://www.wsj.com/articles/saudi-arabia-considers-nuclear-weapons-to-offset-iran-1430999409.

to achieve by developing their own nuclear stockpile or trying to achieve breakout capacity when it comes to nuclear weapons." In light of Obama's February 2011 decision to turn on longtime American ally Egyptian President Hosni Mubarak, which led to his ouster, Obama's decision to remove all American combat troops from Iraq, and his 2013 refusal to enforce his own red line against Syria's use of chemical weapons, what makes Obama think GCC countries trust American assurances?

3. Goldberg asked whether, given what the president has called their "venomous anti-Semitism," the Iranians "can be counted on to be entirely rational." Obama responded that to maintain power and overcome their economic troubles, the Iranians will "strike an agreement on their nuclear program" because antisemitism "doesn't preclude you from being rational." Yet even as the Third Reich was collapsing, Hitler deprived his army of resources by continuing to round up Jews and transport them by train to extermination camps. On what does Obama base his optimism about the rationality of antisemitic dictators?
4. Obama told Goldberg that Netanyahu's statement in the days before Israel's March 17 parliamentary elections—that "a Palestinian state would not happen under his watch"—and the prime minister's election day portrayal of Arab citizens as "an invading force that might vote," along with his insinuation "that this should be guarded against," not only violated Israel's commitment to equality but should also have "foreign-policy consequences." Does Obama not understand that (a) many Israelis who favor a two-state solution nonetheless agree with their prime minister that regional turmoil makes its realization unfeasible in the near term; (b) Netanyahu did *not* portray Arab citizens as an

invading force that might vote but rather as a constituency whose votes would strengthen his opponents, and therefore he urged not the suppression of the Arab vote but a final push to the polls by his supporters; and (c) that Netanyahu's portrayal, though crude, differs little from the overtly ethnic appeals made in US politics all the time, including on Obama's behalf?

5. In the Dayan interview, the president acknowledged that after the election, Netanyahu reaffirmed his commitment to the long-term goal of a Palestinian state and apologized for his remark about Arab voters.[3] But Obama nevertheless questioned Netanyahu's sincerity: "I think that it is difficult to simply accept at face value the statement made after an election that would appear to look as if this is simply an effort to return to the previous status quo in which we talk about peace in the abstract, but it's always tomorrow, it's always later." Why does Obama assert that postelection statements, made after the battle has been decided and the dust has settled, should be dismissed, while statements made in the frantic final days of a fiercely contested race reflect a political leader's deepest and most credible views?
6. The president stressed to Dayan "the necessity to resolve" the conflict between Israel and the Palestinians. Why does President Obama think that the Israeli-Palestinian conflict is more destabilizing than the manifold conflicts shaking the Middle East—the Syrian civil war, which has killed more than 220,000 and produced a flood of more than a million refugees into Lebanon and similar numbers into Jordan; the

---

3 Barack Obama, "Obama Talks on Israeli TV about Netanyahu, Israel and David Blatt," interview by Ilana Dayan, *Jewish Journal,* June 2, 2015, https://jewishjournal.com/news/united-states/171601.

conquests of ISIS in Iraq; the Iran-backed Houthi rebellion in Yemen; Egypt's war against Muslim extremists in the Sinai Peninsula; and Libya's descent into chaos? And why does Obama think that the Israeli-Palestinian conflict alone is subject to near-term resolution?

7. Like Goldberg, Dayan did not mention Palestinian Authority President Mahmoud Abbas, nor did Obama refer to him. By largely ignoring the PA, both interviews gave the impression that Obama believes that Netanyahu presents the major impediment to peace. Wouldn't showing an appreciation of the substantial obstacles to peace presented by Abbas and the Palestinians help Obama persuade Israelis that he understands the complexity of their acute security challenges?
8. Obama implied to Dayan that one "practical consequence" of what he deems Netanyahu's failure to pursue a Palestinian state is that the United States may refrain from vetoing Security Council resolutions aimed at imposing a settlement to the conflict with the Palestinians. The president also said that he sought to "create some building blocks of trust and progress." What are Obama's grounds for supposing that breaking with almost 50 years of American policy—by repudiating UN Security Council resolutions 242 and 338, which call for the parties to negotiate a settlement—would do anything but impair trust and obstruct progress?
9. Obama reiterated to Dayan his displeasure at Netanyahu's decision to address Congress earlier this year. "I think it's fair to say," Obama opined, "that if I showed up at the Knesset without checking with the prime minister first, if I had negotiated with Mr. Herzog, that there would be a sense of some protocols that had been breached." Did Obama consult with Netanyahu before he went over his head to address the Israeli people directly on prime-time

> television, and did Obama give tacit approval for his former political consultants to work to defeat Netanyahu's party in the March elections?

We should be grateful to Jeffrey Goldberg and Ilana Dayan for obtaining answers from President Obama about Israel and the Middle East that illuminate what must be asked in the next round of questions to properly evaluate the president's stance toward Israel and US policies in the region.

4

WHY ISRAELI RULE OF THE GOLAN HEIGHTS IS LAWFUL—AND WISE

February 19, 2016

TEL AVIV—In exercising its right of self-defense during the Six-Day War, Israel seized from Syria the Golan Heights, a strategically important plateau that rises sharply from the eastern bank of the Sea of Galilee to a height of more than 3,000 feet and looms over northeastern Israel. Since June 1967 a consensus has prevailed in the international community, including the United States, that the Golan is occupied territory.

The Syrian civil war, which has raged for almost five years, has done little to disturb the consensus. But the chaos in Syria has weighty legal and political ramifications that should impel the international community, starting with Washington, to revise its understanding of the Golan's status.

Modern Syria, which was born in 1946, has ceased to exist. Bashar al-Assad—who hails from the minority Alawite community, an offshoot of Shia Islam—retains the title of president of Syria, though he now controls less than 25 percent of the country. Despite recent advances by government troops, the Islamic State and other Sunni Islamists continue to dominate much of the territory Assad once governed.

Assad's quest to retain power has produced carnage of epic proportions. When the dictator moved to crush the antiregime, prodemocracy protests that broke out in Syria in early 2011, the country's population numbered approximately 22 million. Since then violence has taken at least 250,000 lives, with more recent reports putting the figure significantly higher. Between 1 million and 1.5 million people have been wounded. More than 5 million refugees have fled to neighboring countries and to Europe. The *Economist* estimated in September 2015 that an additional 7 million people have been forced from their homes but remain within Syria's official borders. The United Nations Office for the Coordination of Humanitarian Affairs believes that more than 13 million Syrians need humanitarian assistance.

Few informed observers think that a functioning nation-state can be reconstructed out of the warring Alawite, Shia, Sunni, Kurd, and Druze factions into which Syria has collapsed. The termination of peace talks in Geneva, shortly after they began in early February, suggests that much blood is still to be spilled.

Foreign funds and fighters sustain the killing. With much of the Syrian army having crumbled, Assad is propped up by Iran-backed Hezbollah fighters from Lebanon, the newly cash-flush Iranians who are pocketing $100 billion or more as a result of the US-brokered deal over their nuclear program, and the Russians, whose air power has inflicted considerable damage on Assad's enemies. Saudi Arabia continues to support Sunni rebels.

In these dramatically transformed circumstances, Israel has the strongest legal claim to the Golan Heights. Its political claim is stronger still.

Until the Six-Day War, Syria used a heavily fortified Golan as a platform to fire at Israeli villages below. Damascus also permitted the Palestinian Liberation Organization to use the Golan as a staging ground for terrorism. In the immediate aftermath of the Six-Day War, Israel offered to negotiate the status of the territories it had seized, which included the West Bank from Jordan and the Gaza Strip and Sinai Peninsula from Egypt. Syria, along with Israel's other Arab neighbors, emphatically rejected the offer.

In December 1981 the Knesset applied Israeli law to the approximately 500 square miles of the Golan Heights under Israeli control. Syria, Jordan, and Egypt promptly accused Israel of unlawfully annexing the territory. Much of the Arab world followed suit. The Europeans also regarded the move as contrary to international law. The Reagan administration supported UN Security Council Resolution 497, which declared Israel's action "null and void and without international legal effect." The administration, however, vetoed a Security Council proposal to impose sanctions on Israel.

Since 1992 four Israeli prime ministers—center-left Yitzhak Rabin and Ehud Barak, centrist Ehud Olmert, and right-wing Benjamin Netanyahu—have sought, to varying degrees, to achieve peace with Syria in exchange for withdrawing from parts or all of the Golan Heights. All initiatives proved futile. In the meantime the Golan has become a thriving site of agriculture, industry, and tourism.

In addition to approximately 20,000 Jewish Israelis, the Golan is home to about 20,000 Druze, who speak Arabic and practice their own distinctive religion. The Golan Druze reside in four towns in the northernmost part of the territory. Unlike the Druze living in the Galilee region of pre-1967 Israel, who are citizens and serve in the army, the vast majority of Golan Druze declined Israeli citizenship. Since the Syrian civil war, however, they have increasingly viewed life in Israel as preferable to the alternative.[1] Today it is rare to see a picture of Assad in a Golan Druze restaurant or store, although some still hang in private homes.

---

1 Judy Maltz, "Not Much Sympathy for Syrian Refugees among Golan Druze," *Haaretz*, September 24, 2015, https://www.haaretz.com/2015-09-24/ty-article/.premium/not-much-sympathy-for-syrian-refugees-among-golan-druze/0000017f-e17c-d804-ad7f-f1fe78540000.

At a restaurant on the edge of the town of Majdal Shams, which lies at the foot of the snowcapped Mount Hermon, a veteran Golan Druze tour guide explained to me that there were two main reasons for his community's historic support for Assad. First, the president of Syria has provided protection for Syrian Druze against Islamic State jihadists, who see the Druze as infidels. Second, the Golan Druze fear that should Israel strike a deal with Syria, Assad would punish them for embracing Israeli rule. He noted, however, that younger Druze are increasingly open in their preference for Israel.

He also stressed that his people generally regard the question of who should rule the Golan as a matter for Syria and Israel to decide. And then, with a shining smile, my Druze companion, who was in his midtwenties when Israel took the Golan in 1967 and thus has living memories of life under Syrian authority, added that he was quite confident that there is not another group in Israel, including the Jews, who have life as good under the Israeli government as do the Golan Druze.

Meanwhile, Israelis across the political spectrum realize that had a return of the Golan been negotiated, Islamic State jihadists would now control the plateau. The Golan Heights, moreover, does not raise the difficult questions for Israelis posed by the West Bank and its restive population of approximately 2.8 million Palestinians because the Golan Druze are a small community pleased with their condition and entitled by law to full Israeli citizenship.

A few voices in Israel are calling for international recognition of Israel's sovereignty over the Golan. Former Cabinet Secretary Zvi Hauser argues that Israel should launch "a constructive dialogue with the international community over a change in Middle Eastern borders and recognition of Israeli rule on the Golan Heights, as part of the global interest in stabilizing the region."[2]

---

2 Zvi Hauser, "A Historic Opportunity for Israel in the Golan Heights," *Haaretz*, July 3, 2015, https://www.haaretz.com/opinion/2015-07-03/ty-article/.premium/an-historic-opportunity-in-the-golan/0000017f-f328-d487-abff-f3fe3e160000.

Retired Israeli General Amos Yadlin, now head of Tel Aviv University's Institute for National Security Studies, maintains that in the aftermath of a flawed Iran deal, the United States would advance its own interests and those of Israel by "promoting recognition of Israel's sovereignty over the Golan Heights." This step, Yadlin told me, would establish a salutary precedent in a region racked by religious and sectarian wars. Last century's borders are not holy, he emphasized, and in sorting out contemporary disputes borders should be adjusted to security exigencies and demographic realities.

But is such adjustment lawful?

Following World War II, international law prohibited the acquisition of territory by force, even in the case of a defensive war. The general tendency is to preserve existing boundaries.

What happens, however, when the party with the claim favored by international law disintegrates? The precedents are few and ambiguous. However, James Crawford's authoritative work, *Brownlie's Principles of Public International Law*, eighth edition, explains that while clear title to land defeats possession, equivocal title creates room for claims based on possession. Syria's disintegration renders title over the Golan equivocal.

Israel's territorial claim arises in part from the principle of "effective occupation," which provides that territory can be acquired through the exercise of sovereign power on a peaceful and extended basis. Israeli law has applied to the Golan for almost 35 years, and Israel has exercised authority in a manner that suits all the residents of the territory.

Moreover, public international law favors stability, order, and peace; it aims to avoid resolutions that expose individuals to death or injury. Accordingly, it should prefer Israeli sovereignty over the Golan to the grim alternatives for the Golan Druze: the tyrannical rule of Shia Islamist Iran's puppet Assad or the tyrannical rule of Islamic State Sunnis.

The international consensus that the Golan belongs to Syria no longer fits the facts and the law. Nor does it coincide with America's interest in checking the spread of Islamist violence throughout the Middle East and in bolstering a democratic ally. At the first opportunity, unlikely to come before the next president's inauguration in January 2017, the United States should affirm Israel's lawful and just exercise of sovereignty over the Golan Heights and urge the international community, particularly US allies in Europe and the Middle East, to do the same.

5

ISRAEL'S "SORROW OF THE LEFT"

March 24, 2016

TEL AVIV—Those on the left of Israeli politics increasingly express fears that the liberal and democratic country that their spiritual forebears built is slipping from their hands.

Earlier this month center-left *Haaretz* columnist Ari Shavit published an impassioned outcry capturing the growing distress and anger I have heard in conversations over the last year with affluent and well-educated residents of Tel Aviv. Shavit takes great pride in Zionism's achievement in creating a state infused with "unequaled passion, creativity and vitality." But Prime Minister Benjamin Netanyahu's government leaves him feeling "ashamed" and with a sense of "deep disgrace."

Among those in power, Shavit sees nothing but "ignorant hooligans" and "boorish" and "uncultured" people who are "smashing and shattering everything precious and sublime" in the country. He himself refuses to surrender to the night that he believes has "descended on Jerusalem" and the forces of darkness that "cover the land." But his affirmation that "true Zionism will rise up" against the political right that he blames for all this smacks more of desperation than optimism.

To better understand the causes of the left's despair, I sought out Yaron London, the host of the popular daily current affairs TV program *London & Kirschenbaum*. A fixture in Israeli media—as radio and TV broadcaster, print journalist, songwriter, actor, and filmmaker for some 50 years and going strong—London is a man of the left who is inspiringly liberal in the old-fashioned sense of the term. He is distinguished by a skepticism of his own side and curiosity about the other side. Both the skepticism and the curiosity are nourished by a sense of humor rooted in sympathy for the foibles and charms of real people.

In a lengthy and wide-ranging conversation in his comfortable apartment on a quiet Tel Aviv street, London rejected the notion that freedom and democracy are under assault in Israel. While he was acutely worried about the growing gap between rich and poor, London insisted that freedom of expression here has never been more robust.

Nonetheless, and without a hint of acrimony, he identified a half-dozen sources of what he dubbed the "sorrow of the left."

First, long-term demographic trends are working against the left. The Israeli right—which encompasses Jews from Arab countries, immigrants from the former Soviet Union, the deeply religious, the less educated, and the poor—has a significantly higher birth rate than the left, whose members generally trace their ancestry to Europe and, for the most part, are better educated, more secular, and more prosperous.

Second, the left views the more than 400,000 Israelis living in the West Bank as having created an all-but-irreversible political reality that will prevent the Jewish state from disentangling itself from more than 2.5 million Palestinians who do not want to live in Israel and to whom most Israelis do not want to grant citizenship.

Third, Israeli and Palestinian negotiating positions are so distant that it appears there is no near-term prospect "to establish something that resembles peace," let alone a two-state solution.

Fourth, the violence and fanaticism in the Middle East have grown so terrible that the national security platform of the center-left has become increasingly indistinguishable from that of the right.

Fifth, the left has been unable to produce "a leader who can compete with Benjamin Netanyahu's mix of intelligence, charisma, and skill in controlling public opinion."

Sixth, the left has internalized the despair of permanent opposition. The right has dominated Israeli politics for almost 40 years with only two exceptions. Yitzhak Rabin, a former general and army chief of staff during the Six-Day War, won election as prime minister in 1992 and led the country until his assassination by a Jewish extremist in 1995. Ehud Barak, a highly decorated former general, headed the government from 1999 to 2001. "When we are repeatedly defeated over a long period of time," London told me, "we gradually lose hope for victory."

It follows from these considerations, he argues, that Israel faces two grim possibilities. One is "stagnation that promises persistent security tension with waves of terror and violent suppression." The other is "annexation of the occupied territories that in the end will produce either institutional apartheid or a democracy in which Arabs will constitute approximately half of the population." The one-state solution "will be unstable and will lead ultimately to civil war."

In these gloomy circumstances, London observes, the question is not why the left is depressed but rather why the right is not. His answer goes to the heart of the matter.

Unlike America, where social and economic issues divide left and right, Israeli politics revolves around conflicting opinions about "the relation to Arabs, the borders of the country, and Israel's character as 'a Jewish and democratic state.'" Whereas the left tends to define the Jewish people as an ethnic group and Israel as a secular state grounded in territory, a common language, and loyalty to agreed-upon social and political arrangements, much of the right, according to London, views the Jewish nation as constituted by religious belief and the Jewish state as subject to religious law and a messianic mission.

The tension between these conceptions, he worries, may be unresolvable. Moreover, contrasting understandings of the Jewish people and Israel, he thinks, explain divergent responses by the left and right to their shared existential anxiety for Israel's survival.

The Israeli left has long believed that the conflict with the Palestinians can be resolved and Arab and Muslim enmity overcome through humane and wise Israeli political leadership. But under pressure from the collapsing Arab state system and the spread of religious war in the region, "this perspective is weakening, and therefore men and women of the left are inclined to think about a private solution," London said. "In almost all 'left-wing' families, you hear talk about emigration or at least doubts about life in the shadow of unending danger and reflections about the advantages contained in citizenship elsewhere." Grandfather to several grandchildren, London makes clear that he does not exempt his own extended family.

In contrast, he suggests, the right draws strength from its religious, or religiously inflected, understanding of Israel's fate. It interprets the establishment of Israel against remarkable odds as proof that the Jewish people will prevail in their ancient homeland while regarding the failure of many on the left to take Israel's side as betrayal of the Jews' divine mission.

London's assessment may underestimate the extent to which liberal and democratic norms have spread, including among the extremely religious. At the same time, his account of the left may neglect the rise of intolerance among progressive elites.

Very much to his credit, London is the first to worry that his observations do injustice to the complexities of Israeli politics. "Everything I told you until now is necessarily afflicted with superficiality and marred by crude generalizations," he stressed. "The boundary lines between the sectors in Israeli society are not drawn with a thick pencil. I spoke of tendencies and inclinations, not hard facts. A skeptic like myself, who has written a great deal and has uttered more than a few predictions that did not come true, must be careful."

The left in Israel—as well as the right in Israel and, come to think of it, both the left and right in America—could use many more affable skeptics endowed with an infectious curiosity like Yaron London.

6

HOW THE IRAN DEAL AIDS HEZBOLLAH, IMPERILS ISRAEL

September 17, 2016

TEL AVIV—In April, Obama administration National Security Advisor Susan Rice told the *Atlantic*'s Jeffrey Goldberg that the Joint Comprehensive Plan of Action (JCPOA) entered into with the Islamic Republic of Iran in July 2015 was "pragmatic and minimalist." According to Rice, "The aim was very simply to make a dangerous country substantially less dangerous."[1]

One year later the Israeli national security establishment continues to debate the Iran deal's merits. Although the debate no longer garners headlines, experts are divided over the reliability of the deal's oversight mechanisms and whether, even if Iran were to scrupulously honor its obligations, the JCPOA would place the Shia theocracy intolerably close to the production of nuclear weapons.

One aspect of the agreement, however, is subject to little dispute in Israel: The JCPOA is not comprehensive. Most here concur that by

1 Jeffrey Goldberg, "The Obama Doctrine," *Atlantic*, April 2016, https://www.theatlantic.com/magazine/archive/2016/04/the-obama-doctrine/471525.

decoupling negotiations over its nuclear program from Iran's funding of terrorism and export of Islamic revolution, and rewarding Iran with tens of billions of dollars of sanctions relief, the agreement has fortified Iran's short-term capacity to destabilize the region.

Although President Obama regularly maintained that the only serious choice the United States confronted was between war with Iran and the deal struck by his team, Israeli Prime Minister Benjamin Netanyahu argued for a third option.

A better deal, Netanyahu insisted in his controversial March 2015 address to Congress, would have forced Iran to make much deeper cuts in its nuclear infrastructure. It would have required Iran to cease its threats to annihilate Israel. And it would have compelled Iran to end its aggression throughout the Middle East—at the moment Supreme Leader Ayatollah Ali Khamenei backs Islamists in Yemen, Iraq, Syria, Lebanon, the West Bank, and the Gaza Strip.

Of special concern to Israel is that under the cover of the JCPOA, Iran continues to arm Hezbollah—Shia Islamist militants headquartered in the south of Lebanon who constitute Israel's largest conventional threat.

Since the 2006 Lebanon War, Hezbollah has increased tenfold its massive arsenal of rockets and missiles targeting Israel.[2] This Iran proxy now possesses more than 100,000 short-range rockets, some with advanced guidance systems recently shipped from Iran, and thousands of precision missiles that can strike all of Israel's major cities and inflict significant damage on Israeli military bases. Hezbollah also boasts a considerable supply of antiaircraft, antiship, and antitank missiles.

By basing its rockets and missiles in towns and villages throughout southern Lebanon, Hezbollah has ensured that Israel's efforts to defend itself will result in thousands of Lebanese civilian casualties and appalling damage to civilian infrastructure. "Both legally and morally," notes

2 Yaakov Amidror, "Lebanon 2006–2016: Deterrence Is an Elusive Concept," Begin-Sadat Center for Strategic Studies, July 10, 2016, https://besacenter.org/lebanon-2006-2016-deterrence-elusive-concept.

international laws of war scholar Geoff Corn, "the cause of these tragic consequences will lie solely at the feet of Hezbollah."[3] Nevertheless, if recent history is a guide, the international community will absolve Hezbollah of guilt while heaping blame on Israel for the likely carnage in Lebanon.

So what is Hezbollah waiting for? Why hasn't it already attacked Israel? Eran Lerman, who stepped down last year as deputy national security advisor to Netanyahu, told me that multiple factors are restraining Hezbollah—at least for now.

First, the high cost Hezbollah paid 10 years ago in the Second Lebanon War established "straightforward deterrence." Although much of the media portrayed the 34-day military conflict as a draw (and Hezbollah leader Hassan Nasrallah hailed it as a "divine victory"), Hezbollah sustained heavy casualties and saw its rocket and missile arsenal severely degraded. A measure of the price Hezbollah paid is the quiet that has prevailed on Israel's northern border for the last decade.

Second, Iran exercises "a derivative deterrence" over Hezbollah, according to Lerman, who is a fellow at the Begin-Sadat Center for Strategic Studies at Bar Ilan University and teaches at Shalem College in Jerusalem. Iran considers the Islamist militant group's fearsome stock of rockets and missiles as essential to its ability to deter an Israeli strike on Iranian nuclear facilities. To deter Israel, Iran must rein in Hezbollah.

Third, Hezbollah is also derivatively deterred by the Syrian civil war. While thousands of Hezbollah combatants in Syria have gained invaluable battlefield experience with sophisticated weapons systems, Hezbollah has also incurred serious losses in the Syrian killing fields. The organization's leaders know that their Sunni adversaries would leap at the opportunity to wipe out a Hezbollah fighting force weakened by war with Israel and, in the process, would exact brutal revenge on a thoroughly exposed Shia civilian population in southern Lebanon.

---

3 Willy Stern, "Missiles Everywhere," *Weekly Standard*, June 10, 2016, https://www.washingtonexaminer.com/magazine/765167/missiles-everywhere.

These multiple levels of deterrence fall far short of ensuring that ordinary misunderstanding and miscalculation, Hezbollah's Islamist fanaticism, and the tumult spread throughout the Gulf and the Levant by fighters loyal to Iran will not in the near term trigger an unintended, ruinous full-scale war between Israel and Hezbollah.

Unfolding events seem to have vindicated Netanyahu's warning that Obama's top foreign policy priority would exacerbate regional instability. Because America's Sunni Arab allies largely agree with Netanyahu's assessment, the deal has also diminished American prestige in the Middle East.

This was a foreseeable consequence of Obama's unconventional version of balance-of-power politics: Instead of strengthening American friends—Israel and moderate Arab states—to restrain a resolute adversary, the president devoted enormous effort to striking an agreement with Iran that empowered Washington's principal regional adversary at the expense of America's local partners. In the effort to strike a "pragmatic and minimalist" deal, the administration has, contrary to Susan Rice's assurances, made Iran—in the short run, at least—more dangerous.

7

TEACHING THE TRADITION OF FREEDOM TO ISRAEL'S ULTRA-ORTHODOX

December 29, 2016

TEL AVIV—Last week I taught an intensive two-day seminar in Jerusalem on the tradition of modern freedom to male *Haredi* ("God fearing" in Hebrew) or ultra-Orthodox Jews. The students were particularly drawn to the challenge of reconciling the claims of individual liberty and democratic self-government with their exacting form of traditional Jewish belief and practice.

The struggle to harmonize freedom and faith is hardly unique to the ultra-Orthodox—or to Israel. But few groups within contemporary liberal democracies experience the conflict as a greater threat than do Israel's ultra-Orthodox. And few of today's liberal democracies have a more urgent interest in facilitating a rapprochement between a deeply pious minority and the essential requirements of a modern nation-state than does Israel.

The students' presence in the seminar—offered by the Tikvah Fund, a New York City–based philanthropic foundation—was anything but routine. The ultra-Orthodox in Israel are largely products of a separate, gender-divided, state-funded educational system. It revolves around the study of Talmud and other sacred Jewish texts while excluding history (including the history of Zionism), literature, political thought, economics, foreign languages, science, and other secular subjects. Because several students spoke little or no English, I conducted the class in Hebrew.

Along with their strictly *yeshiva*, or religious education, the austere dress and self-contained neighborhoods of the ultra-Orthodox are designed to maintain a wall of separation from the main currents of Israeli life. But times are changing, and broader Israeli society exercises its gravitational pull. The seminar participants, for example, belong to the first generation of Israeli ultra-Orthodox who generally speak Hebrew rather than the Yiddish of their Eastern European forebears, whose communities were eradicated in the Holocaust.

The ultra-Orthodox have tended to look upon the rest of Israel with suspicion, while their fellow citizens often view the ultra-Orthodox with rage. The ultra-Orthodox justify their exemption from mandatory military service (Arab citizens are also exempt) and the devotion of large numbers of their adult male population to Talmudic study instead of gainful employment, on the grounds that they safeguard God's law and keep alive a holy tradition. Meanwhile, Israel's secular Jews and many of the country's non-Haredi religious Jews have come to regard the ultra-Orthodox as state-subsidized freeloaders.

The situation is not sustainable over the long term. According to a report issued earlier this year by the Israel Democracy Institute and the Jerusalem Institute for Israel Studies, the ultra-Orthodox constitute about 11 percent of the country's 8.5 million citizens. And they are growing rapidly. Whereas the birth rate in the general population averages 3.1 children per woman, the Haredi community average is 6.9. More than a quarter of all Israeli first-graders are ultra-Orthodox. If current trends continue, by 2059 the ultra-Orthodox will constitute 27 percent of Israel's total population and 35 percent of its Jewish population.

It is therefore good news that "a quiet revolution" has been unfolding among the ultra-Orthodox.[1] Majorities in the Haredi sector affirm pride in Israel. Increasing numbers volunteer for military service. More ultra-Orthodox men and women are enrolling in universities. Employment of ultra-Orthodox men in the economy's technology sector is on the rise.

The students at last week's Tikvah seminar—the youngest in their midtwenties, the oldest in their midfifties—are part of this revolution. While all self-identified as ultra-Orthodox, their appearance and dress ranged from Hasidic-style long, curling sidelocks, full beards, and knee-length black coats in the style of eighteenth-century Polish nobility to neatly cropped hair and casual contemporary fashions. Each wore a black kippah (head covering), although one student, during introductions, announced mischievously that underneath his was a (metaphorical) colorful knitted kippah, which denotes in Israel a welcoming attitude toward modernity. Several of the participants study full-time in yeshivas, some are employed in the private sector, and others work with the government to facilitate better relations with the ultra-Orthodox. A few are pursuing undergraduate degrees.

To launch the seminar, we discussed a popular Israeli short story by award-winning author Etgar Keret about a bus driver (once a mythic figure in Israel) who wanted to be God. The story dramatizes the harm of ideology—a simplifying framework that squeezes the complexities of politics to fit the requirements of some single, exclusive principle. Then we considered Israel's 1948 Declaration of Independence, which draws on a multiplicity of principles springing from a variety of sources—not least the Jewish tradition but also prominently the modern tradition of freedom and individual rights.

---

1 Aron Heller, "In Israel, New Generation of Ultra-Orthodox Jews Integrating," Associated Press, March 19, 2016, https://apnews.com/general-news-1a421da952d342229a2b66f86e4f87a5.

Having established that the responsible exercise of political judgment involves the blending of competing principles and that Israel is founded on the conviction that political freedom is an inseparable dimension of the Jewish state, we turned to our main topic. We explored the foundations of modern political freedom in John Locke's *Second Treatise*, the constitutionalization of that freedom in *The Federalist*, the tensions that arise between democracy and freedom in Alexis de Tocqueville's *Democracy in America*, and freedom of thought and discussion in Mill's *On Liberty*.

The students were particularly intrigued by the limits on the exercise of individual rights that Locke grounded in God's sovereignty, the priority that the US Constitution gives to the protection of religious freedom, and Tocqueville's insistence that religion makes a surpassing contribution to political stability in America by remaining separate from politics.

Passions flared when we turned to Mill. Students readily appreciated the importance of a public sphere—newspapers, broadcast media, and parliament—in which the condition of their freedom of speech was the freedom of speech of all others. After all, the ultra-Orthodox also have interests to advance through the political process. At the same time, they immediately grasped the danger to their way of life posed by the vigorous promotion within the private sphere, embracing their families and communities, of Mill's core conviction—indeed the conviction at the core of all moral and political education worthy of the name—that "he who knows only his own side of the case, knows little of that." Exposing their sons and daughters to Mill's arguments for the sovereign individual, they justly feared, might weaken their children's attachment to the stringent ultra-Orthodox interpretation of God's commandments.

But how can you prepare for effectively exchanging opinions in public life, I asked, without cultivating at home and in civil society curiosity, empathy, and knowledge of history, literature, and moral and political ideas? Doesn't the study of the Talmud itself, I continued, provide support for freedom of thought by encouraging students to explore the other side—indeed the dizzying multiplicity of sides—to the endless arguments that arise in the effort to determine the requirements of Jewish law and apply it to the realities of daily life?

During a break one of the older students approached me. He had a long gray beard and dressed in eighteenth-century garb. He had hardly uttered a word during class. He leaned toward my ear and whispered, "You're saying that living well with—and within—the tradition of freedom is a question of balance?" I nodded and smiled.

Ultimately, both the ultra-Orthodox and broader Israeli society stand to profit from rapprochement. The ultra-Orthodox will benefit from reacquainting themselves with the pleasures and the pride that stem from developing skills valued by the workplace, providing for one's family, and contributing to the national defense. And Israel's secular majority, who, like America's, seek fame and fortune, choreograph their leisure, and chase after quiet time, can enliven their imagination and deepen their understanding of human diversity by learning more about those devoted to fulfilling God's law.

The desired rapprochement repudiates the dogma frequently shared by both sides that freedom and religion are inevitable antagonists. It conceives of them instead as working partners and perhaps indispensable friends.

8

WHY MIDEAST PEACE AMBITIONS MUST BE DIALED BACK

June 17, 2017, discussing Catch-67: The Ideas Behind the Controversy That Is Tearing Israel Apart *by Micah Goodman*

TEL AVIV—The Trump administration is reportedly drafting a document outlining principles to guide negotiations between Israelis and Palestinians.[1] It aims—as did the Clinton, Bush, and Obama administrations—at bringing the protracted conflict to an end.

Trump has called this the "ultimate deal."[2] Having promised to be a disruptive president who would cast aside Washington's worn-out approaches and failed policies, he appears to have set his sights on the great white whale of the American foreign policy establishment—and of the international community.

---

1 Barak Ravid et al., "US Mulls Formulating a Principles Paper on Core Issues of Israeli-Palestinian Conflict," *Haaretz*, June 1, 2017, https://www.haaretz.com/israel-news/2017-06-01/ty-article/.premium/u-s-mulls-principles-on-core-issues-of-me-conflict/0000017f-f64b-d5bd-a17f-f67b00820000.

2 Monica Langley and Gerard Baker, "Donald Trump, in Exclusive Interview, Tells WSJ He Is Willing to Keep Parts of Obama Health Law," *Wall Street Journal*, November 11, 2016, https://www.wsj.com/articles/donald-trump-willing-to-keep-parts-of-health-law-1478895339.

Instead, Trump ought to break with his predecessors by abandoning the ambition to achieve in the near term a final and comprehensive peace. But he should not abandon the Israelis and the Palestinians. In contrast to Presidents Bill Clinton, George W. Bush, and Barack Obama, if he were to pursue a partial and incomplete deal, he would considerably increase the prospects of advancing the interests of both Israelis and Palestinians while restoring American prestige and influence in the region.

In recalibrating its ambitions, the Trump team would benefit, as have Israelis across the political spectrum, from a new book by Micah Goodman. Listening thoughtfully to both sides, he provides a succinct and trenchant guide to the complexities of the internal Israeli argument. And in the process of refining the terms in which his fellow citizens understand the Israeli-Palestinian conflict, Goodman, director of the Academy at Ein Prat and a research fellow at the Shalom Hartman Institute in Jerusalem, exposes the debilitating grip of ideology on the parties and the moral and political superiority of a pragmatic approach to the conflict.

Published in Hebrew last month, *Catch-67: The Ideas Behind the Controversy That Is Tearing Israel Apart* shot to the top of the nonfiction bestseller list here. It received enthusiastic endorsements from former Israel Defense Forces Chief of Staff (and retired Lt. Gen.) Gabi Ashkenazi and from Ruth Gavison, a distinguished professor of law, both associated with the center-left, as well as from retired Gen. Yaakov Amidror, who served as national security advisor to Prime Minister Benjamin Netanyahu and is associated with the center-right. Former Prime Minister Ehud Barak honored the book with a lengthy critique in *Haaretz*, to which Goodman effectively replied. Let's hope *Catch-67* is quickly translated into English.

Goodman explores Israel's searing public debate, which rarely strays far from urgent questions concerning the state's survival and the principles to which it is dedicated, about the West Bank territories of Judea and Samaria that the country captured in defending itself from Jordan's attack 50 years ago this month during the Six-Day War.

The debate, Goodman contends, is marked by a set of paradoxes like the one at the heart of the legendary novel *Catch-22*. Joseph Heller's masterpiece recounts the travails of a World War II US Air Force bombardier who wants to be removed from flying duties because he believes himself to have been driven insane by the mayhem and killing his actions cause. The authorities, however, reject his requests on the grounds that seeking to avoid combat missions is rational and hence evidence of sanity.

Israel's catch-67, according to Goodman, flows from the disconcerting realization that Israel has good reasons for retaining Judea and Samaria as the right wishes and good reasons for withdrawing from it as the left wants. "It has become clear," Goodman writes, "that the right is correct, but it has also become clear that the left is correct."

The left argues that Israel cannot remain a Jewish and democratic state while ruling over the West Bank's more than 2.5 million Palestinians. Unless it withdraws, Israel will destroy its democratic character by denying them citizenship, but it would subvert its Jewish character by granting them citizenship.

The right replies that withdrawal from the West Bank would leave Israel with indefensible borders. Hamas would quickly overrun the Palestinian Authority and establish another Islamist theocracy determined to destroy the Jewish state—this one in Judea and Samaria, the heart of biblical Israel, and overlooking the Jewish state's densely populated coastal plain.

Both left and right are persuasive, concludes Goodman: "The withdrawal that saves Israel from one existential threat produces another existential threat."

Left and right in Israel are similarly persuasive on other crucial issues.

The left, for example, claims that conquest of the West Bank corrupted and continues to corrupt Israeli morals. The right replies that the territories are not conquered but rather are disputed: Palestinians never had a state; Jordan conquered the territory unlawfully in 1948–1949 during Israel's War of Independence, and when Israel tried to return the territories in the immediate aftermath of the Six-Day War, Jordan joined other leading Arab states in issuing at Khartoum the famous "Three Noes"—no peace, no recognition, no negotiations. Goodman distills the important truth in each view: The Palestinian people living under Israeli rule are conquered, but the land on which they live is not.

Jewish identity also argues powerfully for and against withdrawal from the territories. On one hand, the biblical prophets demand one law for all and equal justice for minorities and strangers, which is impossible to implement in the West Bank while maintaining Israel as a Jewish and democratic state. On the other hand, withdrawal from Judea and Samaria sacrifices a key part of Jewish identity while exposing Israel to intolerable security threats.

Finally, Zionism gives rise to clashing claims, both of which are compelling. The Zionist movement drew inspiration from the universal principle that every people is entitled to a homeland, which for Jews means the land of Israel and in particular Judea and Samaria. Yet how then can the Jewish national liberation movement, grounded as it is in the universal principle of national self-determination, justify the subjugation of millions of West Bank Palestinians? Israel's presence in Judea and Samaria, Goodman maintains, both realizes and contradicts the Zionist vision. So does withdrawing from them.

The paradoxes and snares do not end there. The Palestinians, Goodman observes, are caught in the grips of a catch-67 of their own. Israeli agreement to the establishment of a Palestinian state rests on West Bank Palestinians dropping the claim that some 5 million of their brethren around the world have the right to return to Israel and on recognizing Israel as the nation-state of the Jewish people.

But both concessions would violate defining Palestinian commitments. Palestinian national aspirations are bound up with not only ruling themselves in the territory Israel captured from Jordan in 1967 but also acquiring control over all of Israel. Muslim religious law, moreover, forbids the rule of non-Muslims in land, such as all pre-1967 Israel, that Muslims once ruled. "A Palestinian declaration of the end of the conflict and a cessation of demands, therefore, is a betrayal of the refugees and violation of Islamic religious law," Goodman writes. "In order to make peace, the Palestinians would have to commit a religious sin and sin against their national aspirations."

Because of the multiple and maddening catch-67s in which Israelis and Palestinians are enmeshed, Goodman concludes that the conflict between them cannot be solved, at least for now. But it can be transformed from a "fatal problem to a chronic problem."

Goodman sketches two pragmatic options. Both stem from the recognition that no formula exists to fully and finally reconcile both sides' fundamental moral, political, and security claims, and therefore measures must be fashioned that reduce tensions without denying either side's deepest commitments. His core idea is that Israel should take calibrated steps to reduce its control over Palestinian population centers in the West Bank while, for defense purposes, maintaining control over the Jordan River Valley as well as major Israeli settlement blocs. This would increase Palestinian control over their lives while preserving Israeli security.

Another name for the ambition to solve the unsolvable is messianism. Opting instead to ease the conflict between Israel and the Palestinians depends on Israelis on the left and right overcoming their messianic inclinations. It also requires Palestinians to overcome theirs—and American presidents and diplomats to overcome theirs.

9

CALLING OUT THE TELLERS OF ANTI-ISRAEL LIES

October 27, 2017, discussing Industry of Lies: Media, Academia, and the Israeli-Arab Conflict *by Ben-Dror Yemini*

Media coverage of, and academic writings about, Israel routinely betray the intellectual integrity that should govern both. Israel has paid a steep price; the Palestinians perhaps more so.

It would be difficult to quantify precisely the damage inflicted by the omissions, distortions, and accusations that routinely disfigure portrayals of Israel. Still, the steady flow of malicious propaganda posing as news and scholarship poisons the debate about a complex and tragic clash between two peoples. The frequent characterizations of Israel as a moral and political monster—a state supposedly guilty of colonialism, apartheid, and all manner of war crimes and crimes against humanity, including forced population transfer, ethnic cleansing, and genocide—reinforce Palestinian expectations that their demands be met immediately and in full while bolstering Israeli suspicions that they can't get a fair hearing in the court of international public opinion and can't secure a just deal under the international community's auspices. Gross untruths about Israel drive the parties further apart, not only defaming Israel but also setting back the legitimate interests of the Palestinians, whose cause they are contrived to advance.

Emphasizing your side's merits and the other side's defects is only human, and partisan reporting is an old story. The new story is that in service of largely progressive political goals and in stark conflict with their professional obligations to present the facts and tell the truth, Western journalists and professors have erected an edifice of falsehoods about Israel.

To catalog the falsehoods, expose their authors and promulgators, and set the record straight requires prodigious research and painstaking documentation, a grasp of contemporary political realities, and a synoptic, historically informed understanding of the larger Israeli-Arab conflict. With the 2014 publication in Hebrew of *Tasiyat Hashkarim*, which became a bestseller in Israel, journalist Ben-Dror Yemini established that he was the man for the task. His book, *Industry of Lies: Media, Academia, and the Israeli-Arab Conflict,* just appearing in English translation, will prove indispensable to those politicians and policymakers, journalists and professors, and members of the public who understand that getting the story right in the Middle East is inseparable from advancing the cause of peace.

Yemini, with whom I have had the pleasure of discussing Israeli politics for several years, is a columnist at *Yedioth Ahronoth*, Israel's second-most widely read newspaper. A lawyer by training, he also served as opinion-page editor at *Maariv*, another leading outlet. He is counted among a small number of eminent center-to-center-left public intellectuals—including Professor Emeritus Shlomo Avineri, Professor Emerita Ruth Gavison, Professor Yossi Shain, journalist Ari Shavit, and Professor Alexander Yakobson—whom the left often confuses with conservatives because they are proud Zionists.

Unlike the Israeli right, they generally opposed the country's West Bank settlement policy and today, for the most part, object to building outside the large settlement blocs—in effect, small cities that nearly everyone expects to remain under Israel's control. They do not hesitate to criticize the government when it deviates from the liberal and democratic principles on which the country was established while insisting that Israel was properly founded as also, and should remain, the nation-state of the Jewish people. Since the eruption of the Second Intifada in 2001, following Palestinian Authority President Yasser Arafat's flat-out rejection of Israeli Prime Minister Ehud Barak's 2000 Camp David peace proposal, Yemini and those of similar sensibility have highlighted the major obstacles to peace posed by PA intransigence, PA incitement against Israel, and the Sunni and Shia jihadism that pervades Israel's harsh, unstable neighborhood.

Yemini's book deals with these obstacles but focuses on another formidable impediment to easing the conflict: the multitude of lies whose purpose is to delegitimize Israel and place it beyond the pale. Yemini emphasizes that his targets are not imprecise reporting, debatable interpretations, or occasional errors and lapses in judgment but rather demonstrable falsehoods.

The lies, he argues, take several forms.

"The insidious lie" is constructed out of half-truths and suppressed information. For example, in 2010, writing in the *New York Review of Books*, journalist Peter Beinart claimed that Israeli Prime Minister Benjamin Netanyahu "rejects the idea of a Palestinian state." Beinart cited a book by Netanyahu published in 1993—a time when the idea was also rejected by most of the Israeli left, including then-Prime Minister Yitzhak Rabin—while omitting mention of Netanyahu's groundbreaking 2009 Bar-Ilan address, in which he became the first conservative Israeli prime minister to endorse a Palestinian state.

"Lies of proportion" attach terms denoting thoroughgoing evil—say, "apartheid"—to common forms of discrimination that can and should be corrected within the system. Such is the case with the condition of Israel's Arab citizens who, while accorded full civil and political rights, nevertheless face remediable discrimination similar to, and in many cases less severe than, that to which ethnic minorities in European countries are subject. Lies of proportion also include condemnations wildly at odds with transgressions. In 2013, Yemini notes, the UN Human Rights Council "adopted 25 Resolutions, four for all the other countries in the world and 21 against Israel."

"Lies based on true stories" present an inflammatory statement or violent action as if it were representative of the society. It is all too common for reporters and academics to dwell on the outrageous utterances or deeds of fringe figures in Israel while ignoring the country's pluralistic fabric. Yemini calls attention to Israeli versions of popular reality TV shows in which the viewing public votes to determine the winner. Between 2013 and 2015, for example, Israelis chose as champions an Arab Israeli on *Master Chef*, another Arab Israeli on *The Voice*, an Ethiopian Jewish woman on *Big Brother*, and a Filipino foreign worker on *The X Factor.*

"Academic lies" are the work of professors who exploit their university positions and scholarly authority. Yemini quotes Professor Ilan Pappé, a notorious inventor of Israeli crimes who, in a 2004 book, brazenly justified contempt for the historical record: "My bias is apparent despite the desire of my peers that I stick to facts and the 'truth' when reconstructing past realities. I view any such construction as vain and presumptuous." In other words Pappé gives the name reality to scurrilous accusations against the Jewish state based on invented facts.

Then there is the "the Big Lie," which distorts reality so grotesquely that ordinary people assume that nobody would have the effrontery to promulgate the odious claim if it weren't true. "The contemporary version of the Big Lie turns Israel, a country that harms innocent bystanders less than any other party to a conflict of similar proportions, into a state that carries out genocide," writes Yemini. "Meanwhile, terrorists and Hamas members, who publicly announce their intentions to exterminate the Jews, become 'freedom fighters.'"

In a particularly revelatory chapter, Yemini explores the social and economic wellbeing of West Bank and Gaza Palestinians. "Israel's control," Yemini writes, "has not gotten in the way of Palestinian prosperity." To the contrary, citing an array of charts and graphs covering life expectancy, infant mortality, and education, he shows that "by all objective measures," Israel's administration in Gaza, which ended in 2005, and the West Bank, which continues, "only accelerated the rate of development in these areas—despite, not because of, the best efforts of the Palestinian national movement." This has placed Palestinians well ahead of the vast majority of Middle East Arabs.

Imagine how much nearer Palestinians might be today to ruling themselves if our progressive media and academy got in the habit of telling the truth about Israel.

10

AN ISRAELI'S OVERTURE TO HIS PALESTINIAN NEIGHBORS

May 12, 2018, discussing Letters to My Palestinian Neighbor *by Yossi Klein Halevi*

Last month dueling guest opinion pieces marking the seventieth anniversary of Israel's birth (according to the Hebrew calendar) appeared in the United States' two most influential newspapers. The opposing spirits in which the articles were written reflect a recurring asymmetry in the Israeli-Palestinian conflict.

On April 18 in the *New York Times*, Knesset member Ayman Odeh mourned the suffering that Israel's founding inflicted on his people. Head of the Joint List, a coalition of Arab parties that represents the third-largest bloc in Israel's parliament, Odeh asserts that "self-determination for Jews" meant "a catastrophe—'nakba' in Arabic—for Palestinians."

Odeh's enumeration of grievances against Israel is unrelentingly one-sided and all too typical of Arab leaders in Israel, as well as of prominent Palestinians in the West Bank and Gaza. He writes, for example, that because of Israel's War of Independence—during which, Odeh declines to mention, the Jewish state fended off five invading Arab armies that sought its destruction—"in the area around the Mediterranean city of

Haifa, where my family has lived for six generations, only 2,000 Palestinians of a population of 70,000 remained." He adds, "My grandparents, A'bdel-Hai and A'dla, were among them. Their neighbors were expelled and dispossessed, and never allowed to return."

In all, he claims, "More than 400 Palestinian communities were destroyed entirely." He blames Israel for imposing military rule on its Arab citizens until 1966. He condemns a 2011 law that, he states, undertakes to "erase the painful truth of the Nakba" by creating financial penalties for any institution receiving public funding that "mourns the Nakba on the same day as Independence Day." Moreover, "the Israeli educational system perpetuates the Nakba by refusing to teach about Palestinian society before 1948." The government adds to the catastrophe, he asserts, by denying critical infrastructure to Palestinian villages and by imposing "unbearable" travel restrictions on West Bank Palestinians.

To end the Nakba, declares Odeh, Israel must "fully accept" Palestinians' humanity; establish a Palestinian state; acknowledge and rectify the crimes it has perpetrated against Palestinians, which include ensuring justice for Palestinian refugees (by which he seems to mean all 5 million or so descendants in the region of the refugees of 1948); and teach Palestinian history and culture in Israeli schools.

Odeh's tendentious rendition of the facts is to be expected. That he ascribes all fault for the conflict to Israel, identifies no actions that the Palestinians must take to improve their condition, and does not have a good word to say about his country—leaving the impression that his prominent position in the Knesset is an inexplicable aberration from Israel's remorseless oppression of his people—underscores his rancor and intransigence.

In contrast, a spirit of compromise and reconciliation—which, while by no means the norm in Israel, reflects a distinct political tendency—suffuses a *Wall Street Journal* essay Yossi Klein Halevi published a few days before the *Times* ran Odeh's op-ed. Halevi, a senior fellow at the Shalom Hartman Institute in Jerusalem, laments the "maximalist ambitions" on both sides of the conflict. Many Palestinians in the West Bank and the Gaza Strip dream of a Palestinian state governing all the land between the Jordan River and the Mediterranean Sea. Meanwhile, he reports, many right-wing religious Jews who live in the West Bank dream that Israel will one day extend its full sovereignty over Judea and Samaria.

Both dreams, Halevi stresses, are sustained by powerful moral, political, and historical claims. Both dreams, he insists, are ruinous.

Halevi himself agrees with the many Jewish residents of the Israeli-built villages and towns in Judea and Samaria, which encompass the heart of ancient Israel, who maintain that the land on which they dwell is theirs. At the same time, Halevi knows that Israel's rule over the West Bank's nearly 3 million Palestinians, however beneficent and indirect it may one day become, threatens Israel's character as Jewish and democratic. "Reluctantly, painfully," he writes, "I am ready to trade parts of my homeland for a peace that would include recognition of Israel's legitimacy and of the Jewish people's indigenousness in this land." These are, he observes, "concessions that no Palestinian leader has been willing to offer."

In his new book, *Letters to My Palestinian Neighbor*—available online in Arabic for free downloading—Halevi continues his search of many years for common ground. "One of the main obstacles to peace is an inability to hear the other side's story," he writes. Accordingly, his book "is an attempt to explain the Jewish story and the significance of Israel in Jewish identity to the Palestinians who are my next-door neighbors." Stemming in part from his excursions into his neighbors' world to hear the Palestinian and Islamic story, it offers an "invitation to a conversation, in which both sides disagree on the most basic premises." It is a daunting invitation because the interlocutors, Halevi is acutely aware, "are intruders in each other's dreams, violators of each other's sense of home."

Not presuming to speak for anyone other than himself, Halevi offers an invitation to conversation with fellow Jews in Israel and abroad and, indeed, with all those who—whether out of humanitarian, geopolitical, or religious concerns—wish to understand the prospects for easing the Israeli-Palestinian conflict. (Disclosure: Halevi's book tour is supported by the Paul E. Singer Foundation, as is The Public Interest Fellowship, for which I serve as director of studies.)

Halevi's letters charm, inspire, and illuminate. They embody his religious faith; his imaginative sympathies for the yearnings and fears of a neighbor who, he knows, is in many cases an adversary; his bracing sense of justice; his unbending commitment to the flourishing of the Jewish people and the Jewish state; and his realistic assessment of the complex imperatives of Israeli national security.

With gentle pride he explains to his Palestinian neighbor the basics of Jewish history, belief, and practice. He examines the similarities between Judaism and Islam—the two Abrahamic religions built around sacred laws—and major differences, not least Judaism's encouragement of wrestling with God's commands and Islam's focus on submission to Allah. Halevi recounts his journey from Brooklyn, where he grew up to be a strident, right-wing religious nationalist; his decision as a twenty-something in the 1980s to immigrate to Israel; and his gradual realization as an Israeli citizen that the holy land he loves and believes by right belongs to the Jewish people must be divided with the Palestinians not only as a demand of justice but also for the sake of the Jewish people whom he loves still more than he loves the land.

Halevi warmly conveys his desire to one day host in his home the Palestinians who live just beyond and below his apartment in Jerusalem's French Hill neighborhood and whom he hears at prayer and glimpses from above the security barrier that separates them. He tells of his inspiring encounters with Islam and Muslim religious leaders. He describes with awe contemporary Israel's contradictory longings: to be a normal nation like all other nations and to be an exceptional nation, a light unto the nations. As the son of a refugee from Hitler's war to exterminate the Jews, he elucidates the Holocaust's profound influence, even as the last survivors pass away, on Israeli hearts and minds.

A single overriding political purpose informs Halevi's eloquent overtures to his Palestinian neighbor. It is to convince the two sides that their conflicting claims to rule over the entire land oblige both to accept "heartbreaking concessions" such that each will "exercise national sovereignty in only a part of the land."

Which concessions exactly? What parts of the land precisely?

Halevi does not say. The answers depend on the conversation that his letters aim to foster.

And the conversation depends on both sides summoning the spirt of compromise guided by principle and of reconciliation rooted in strength that Halevi's book exemplifies.

11

ISRAEL CAN EASE GAZA TENSIONS, BUT SO MUST THE UN

June 8, 2018

TEL AVIV—In mid-May freelance journalist Ahmed Abu Artema, an organizer of "Gaza's Great Return March," emphasized in a *New York Times* op-ed the peaceful intentions of a movement that has sparked violence since late March and led to dozens of Palestinians killed and thousands injured by Israel in defense of its border. In fact, the movement's very name proclaims a warlike ambition. The "Great Return March," a journey from Gaza to Palestinians' supposedly true homes in the sovereign state of Israel, reflects the dream of abolishing the Jewish state.

This dream is the root cause of the humanitarian disaster suffered by Gazans and of Iran-backed Hamas's new round of war—employing flaming kites to set ablaze Israeli fields on a near-daily basis and launching terrorist infiltration to commit atrocities against Israel's civilian population.

The seed that grew into "Gaza's Great Return March," according to Artema, was planted in December when President Trump announced—in accordance with a decades-old congressional resolution, the Jerusalem Embassy Act of 1995—that the United States would move its embassy from Tel Aviv to Israel's capital city. This, asserted Artema, deepened the wound he feels when he looks across the fence that separates Gaza from Israel and sees what he believes to be occupied Arab land.

The international community stokes Gazans' ruinous belief that Israel belongs to them and fuels their delusive dream of return. On May 18, for example, the UN Human Rights Council again improperly intervened in the Israeli-Palestinian conflict in favor of Hamas. By an overwhelming margin—29 countries in favor, two against (the United States and Australia), and 14 abstaining—the Human Rights Council authorized an investigation into the violence arising from the Gaza demonstrations, while, in advance of the investigation, it "condemns the disproportionate and indiscriminate use of force by the Israeli occupying forces against Palestinian civilians."

Never mind that Israel, having withdrawn from the territory in 2005, does not occupy Gaza and resorted to force in the recent confrontations only after issuing abundant warnings and in manifestly legitimate defense of its territorial integrity. The council's gratuitous and entirely foreseeable action usurped Israel's right and interfered with its responsibility under international law to investigate allegations of misconduct by its military. The one-sided resolution, moreover, airbrushed Hamas's unlawful dispatch of combatants dressed as civilians into the front lines of the border-fence demonstrations with the intent of breaching Israeli defenses.

Meanwhile, the United Nations Relief and Works Agency (UNRWA) persists in encouraging Gazan and West Bank Palestinians—along with Palestinians living in Lebanon, Syria, Jordan, and throughout the Middle East and around the world—to see themselves as refugees endowed with an eternal right of return to Israel. In December 1949 the United Nations established UNRWA to provide care for local Arabs displaced by the war five Arab armies launched against Israel following its Declaration of Independence in May 1948. UNRWA, however, has deviated greatly from its original mandate. With the international community's blessing, it has turned itself into the only UN organization dedicated to restoring homes and lands not to the people who left them but to their descendants.

All refugees around the globe apart from Palestinians come under the jurisdiction of the UNHCR, the UN Refugee Agency, formally known as the United Nations High Commissioner for Refugees. The UNHCR's overarching goal is to transform refugees into citizens. First it tries to repatriate them. If that fails, it promptly turns to resettling and integrating them elsewhere.

In stark contrast to the UNHCR, UNRWA seeks to return Palestinians, most of whom by now were not born in Israel, to the land of their parents and grandparents while neglecting for several generations Palestinian resettlement and integration elsewhere. Unlike the UNHCR, UNRWA treats refugee status as inheritable. That's why, despite there being no more than about 700,000 Arabs who left their homes in 1948 and 1949 during Israel's War of Independence, UNRWA today recognizes more than 5 million Palestinians as refugees.

By nurturing this dream of return, the international community perpetuates the Israeli-Palestinian conflict. Repeatedly assured by diplomats and intellectuals that their people are blameless for the conflict and possess a "right of return," Palestinian leaders refuse pragmatic accommodations. Systematically encouraged to believe that their grievances are Israel's fault, Palestinians reject compromise. Relieved of accountability for violating the laws of war, they make human shields of their noncombatants and make military targets of Israeli noncombatants.

Improving Gazans' lives depends on the transformation of Palestinian political culture, and of the international community's political culture that enables Palestinian belligerence and intransigence.

Israel, however, cannot pin its fate on such improbable developments. As a matter of self-interest, it must look for ways to reduce tensions with Hamas and diminish Gazans' suffering.

Gaza is a crisis waiting to explode. A narrow slice of land a little more than twice the size of Washington, DC, it is bordered to the west by the Mediterranean, to the north and east by Israel, and to the south and west by Egypt's Sinai Peninsula. About 45 percent of the approximately 1.8 million Gazan Palestinians are under age 15; about 66 percent are under age 25. Since seizing control of Gaza in 2007, Iran-backed Hamas has established an Islamist despotism whose overriding purpose is Israel's destruction. Nevertheless, Gaza remains dependent on Israel for water, electricity, and other humanitarian necessities.

That's in part because Israel imposed a land, sea, and air blockade on Gaza to prevent Hamas from importing rockets, missiles, and other weapons. It is also because of harsh controls instituted by the Egyptians at the Rafah Border Crossing, which separates Gaza from the Sinai Peninsula.

Three times in the last 10 years—winter 2008–2009, autumn 2012, and summer 2014—Israel undertook military operations inside Gaza to counter Hamas mortar, rocket, and missile attacks on its civilian population. With the advent of the Iron Dome air defense system, Israel has gone a long way toward neutralizing the threat from Gazan projectiles. So Hamas has diverted a substantial portion of the building materials arriving in Gaza to constructing tunnels into Israel for terrorist attacks.

Israel has countered by installing an underground antitunnel wall. It is also building an underwater fence to prevent attacks from the sea. Hamas's response is the Great March of Return.

A consensus has formed in Israel stretching from beyond the center-right to beyond the center-left that there is little to do in the short term to improve the situation. That's probably right.

But Israel should pursue the little it can do energetically. Even as it ensures that Hamas pays the price for acts of war, Israel must maintain a flow of basic goods to Gaza. And it must take advantage of opportunities, few and far between though they may be, to develop commerce and industry there.

Egypt can help. As member of Knesset Anat Berko (Likud) told me, Cairo should allow more goods and individuals to pass through the Rafah Border Crossing. Sinai's El Arish International Airport, less than 50 miles away, should become a Gaza hub.

The United States can help. It should bring diplomatic pressure and financial incentives to bear on the Egyptians to ease restrictions on Gaza.

And the international community should do its part. By ceasing to encourage vain hopes and absurd expectations, it can help Gazans emancipate themselves from their self-destructive dream of return and replace it with the resolve to build prosperous lives on the land they inhabit in the here and now.

12

CRAFTING A CONSTRUCTIVE GAZA POLICY

December 27, 2018

TEL AVIV—"The situation for 1.5 million Palestinians in the Gaza Strip is worse now than it has ever been since the start of the Israeli military occupation in 1967," according to "The Gaza Strip: A Humanitarian Implosion." The report, published by a coalition of nongovernment organizations, describes an alarming shortage of humanitarian and commercial supplies in Gaza. Drinking water and electricity fall well below demand. Sewage flows into the Mediterranean Sea. With unemployment around 40 percent, the economy is collapsing.

Nevertheless, the report professes optimism: "The current situation in Gaza is man-made, completely avoidable and, with the necessary political will, can also be reversed." The authors advocate formal condemnation of Israel's blockade, greater pressure on Israel to open border crossings and increase the supply of fuel and other necessities, and resumption of a peace process that will "insist that the Israeli government and the Palestinian Authority as well as Hamas and other Palestinian armed groups adhere to their human rights and international humanitarian law commitments."

Sponsored by Oxfam—along with Amnesty International UK, CARE International UK, and other aid organizations—the report appeared in 2008.

Ten years later, many—including Israel's defense establishment—believe that Gaza's humanitarian crisis is even worse. In 2018, as in 2008, many international observers adopt the Oxfam-report perspective on what has gone wrong. Ignoring the principal "man-made" cause of Gaza suffering, they primarily blame Israel or assume a moral equivalence between Iran-backed Hamas's determination to attack Israel and Israel's determination to defend itself.

Gaza's rehabilitation would not only benefit its long-suffering Palestinian residents. It would also improve Israeli security and enhance regional stability. And it would serve American interests by enabling Israel and pragmatic Arab states to collaborate more effectively in the struggle against Iranian aggression. But Hamas's interest in maintaining its iron-fisted theocratic rule and its jihadist ambition to eradicate the Jewish state, notwithstanding Israel's 2005 withdrawal to pre-June 1967 borders, limit options for Israel, pragmatic Arab states, and the United States.

Hamas continues to acquire rockets and missiles to bombard Israeli civilians, and to construct cross-border tunnels to perpetrate atrocities. That's the reason Israel must maintain its blockade and has undertaken three major military incursions into Gaza over the last 10 years.

Hamas continues to transform Gaza's cities into battlefields by positioning headquarters, military bases, weapons caches, and rocket launchers near, in, or under civilian buildings. That's the reason the fighting into which Hamas has drawn Israel has injured and killed thousands of Palestinian noncombatants and inflicted substantial damage on basic infrastructure.

Hamas continues to foment hatred of Israel through local media and Gaza's schools, to use Palestinian misery as a tool of radicalization, and to persuade Gazans that what is now Israel rightfully belongs to them and will someday, through force of arms, be theirs. That's the reason Hamas was able last spring to assemble thousands of fighters, women, and children along the border, week after week, threatening to breach Israel's security fence. It's also why Hamas could mobilize Gazans throughout the summer to cast aloft incendiary balloons and kites, which, blown into Israel by the sea breeze, produced extensive damage by setting Israel's fields ablaze. And that's the reason Israel—which, like any self-respecting nation, must safeguard its borders and prevent its territory from going up in flames—has been compelled to use force against a mixture of combatants and ostensible noncombatants, whose wounds and corpses Hamas exploits to mobilize recruits and elicit international support.

Were it not for Hamas's resolute acts of war—because they target Israeli civilians and use Palestinian civilians as shields, they constitute flagrant violations of international law—Gazans would not face today an appalling scarcity of electricity and potable water, rivers of untreated sewage polluting beaches and groundwater and spreading parasites, and a decimated economy.

The authors of "Ending Gaza's Perpetual Crisis: A New US Approach," published this month, aim to change course.

A joint product of two blue-chip Washington think tanks, the centrist Center for a New American Security (CNAS) and the center-left Brookings Institution, the report maintains that over the last decade, the United States has pursued a permanent status agreement between Israel and the Palestinian Authority at the expense of Gaza, from which Hamas expelled the PA in 2007. The CNAS-Brookings report calls for "a proactive US policy" to extricate Gaza's nearly 2 million residents from poverty and deprivation, to advance Israeli-Palestinian peace, and to reduce conflict in the Sinai Peninsula where, since 2011, the Egyptian government has battled ISIS-inspired jihadists.

The new approach consists of stabilizing Gaza through humanitarian relief and reintegrating it into the PA so that Gazan and West Bank

Palestinians can cooperate to establish an independent state embracing both territories. To achieve these objectives, argues the report, the United States must undertake "vigorous diplomacy." The extensive multilateralism the report envisages encompasses not only Hamas, the PA, and Israel but also the UN Special Coordinator for the Middle East Peace Process, Egypt, Saudi Arabia, the United Arab Emirates, Qatar, Europe, Jordan, and Turkey.

The report elaborates several useful recommendations—involving cooperation among Hamas, the PA, the United States, Israel, and the international community—for increasing water and electricity in Gaza and for improving waste management. It laudably decouples these practical, near-term measures for relieving the worst of the humanitarian crisis from the attainment of a comprehensive peace.

Yet despite its ambition to break with the mistakes of the past, the CNAS-Brookings report embodies the old approach, the same one that informed Obama administration Secretary of State John Kerry's frenetic and failed diplomacy.

First, by offering anodyne formulations about the "cycle of violence" that blur the difference between Hamas's desire to destroy Israel and Israel's determination to defend itself, the report obscures the abiding sources of Gaza's humanitarian crisis.

Second, while acknowledging the "abnormal complexity of the situation," the report envisages a "coordinated diplomatic effort" that is abnormally complex. It is doubtful that the PA leadership—which rejected peace proposals advanced by President Bill Clinton and Israeli Prime Minister Ehud Barak at Camp David in 2000, by Israeli Prime Minister Ehud Olmert in 2008, and by Kerry in 2013–2014—will cooperate with the elaborate scheme devised at CNAS and Brookings to end the Gaza crisis. The report also glosses over the political hurdles faced by the many other countries with conflicting concerns, including Israel, to which the report assigns crucial roles. And the report fails to identify any element in Hamas's mindset or strategic outlook to which diplomats might appeal to induce it to relinquish administrative power, allow the PA back into Gaza, and combine security forces—all of which CNAS-Brookings experts deem essential.

Third, the report blames the Trump administration for damaging relations with the PA by recognizing Jerusalem as Israel's capital, moving the American embassy there, and cutting aid to the PA and to UNRWA (a UN organization that provides Palestinians social, economic, and educational services). But Jerusalem is Israel's capital. Pretending otherwise encourages Palestinians to indulge unrealistic expectations and advance extravagant demands. And coddling the PA and overlooking UNRWA's corruption and anti-Israel propagandizing have contributed to the decades-long blighting of Gaza.

Good intentions and political will are rarely enough. To craft a constructive policy for Gaza, as elsewhere, the United States must resist fantasizing about the interests that ought to motivate regional actors and instead grasp those that do.

13

BRIDGING THE RELIGIOUS-SECULAR DIVIDE

May 19, 2019, discussing The Philosophic Roots of the Religious-Secular Divide *by Micah Goodman (subsequently translated into English as* The Wondering Jew: Israel and the Search for Jewish Identity*)*

Of the many causes of political polarization in the United States, the conflict between religion and secularism is the oldest and deepest. Easing this conflict, desirable for its own sake, also stands a chance of tempering the increasingly entrenched enmity in our politics between right and left.

Americans' stance on religion today often correlates with their location on the political spectrum. Although men and women of the right may hold secular views and men and women of the left can be found in houses of worship, practitioners of traditional faith tend to embrace conservative ideas, while convinced secularists are more likely to congregate in progressive circles.

At least one opinion, however, transcends the religious-secular divide: The religious and the secular typically share the conviction that between the two communities lies an all but unbridgeable gulf. This reinforces the belief common to contemporary conservatives and progressives that they inhabit separate and incurably hostile worlds.

But what if the conviction that religion and secularism are intractable adversaries is mistaken? What if a certain disabling dogmatism afflicts both the religious spirit and the secular spirit? What if reexamination of traditional religious sources and of seminal works of secularism reveals that both teach an openness, even an imperative, to consider respectfully and learn from the achievements of the other?

My friend Micah Goodman explores these enticing possibilities in his splendid new book about religion and secularism in Israel. The implications of his argument are far reaching.

Published last month in Hebrew and not yet translated into English, the book nevertheless bears on its title page an English rendering of its title as *The Philosophic Roots of the Religious-Secular Divide.*[1] This captures an important dimension of Goodman's contribution. But a more literal translation, and one closer to the spirit of the book, would be *Return Without Faith: Another Secularism and Another Religiosity.*

A research fellow at the Shalom Hartman Institute in Jerusalem, Goodman has developed an expertise in diagnosing false dichotomies that have taken hold in the Jewish state and in showing Israelis how to extricate themselves from those intellectual traps. In his 2017 Israeli bestseller *Catch-67: The Ideas Behind the Controversy That Is Tearing Israel Apart*, he argued that debate about the territory that Israel captured from Jordan in the Six-Day War had reached an impasse because both the left and the right are correct.

The left is correct, contended Goodman, that remaining in the West Bank produces an existential threat. Israel can't preserve both its Jewish and its democratic character if it continues to rule indefinitely over more than 2.5 million West Bank Palestinians. Over the long term, denying them citizenship would subvert Israel's democratic character, while offering them citizenship would erode its Jewish character.

1 Goodman's book was subsequently translated into English and published as *The Wondering Jew: Israel and the Search for Jewish Identity* (Yale University Press, 2020).

The right is also correct, maintained Goodman, that withdrawing from Judea and Samaria (the biblical names, preferred by the right, for the West Bank) presents an existential threat. Returning to the pre-June 1967 borders would undercut Israel's ability to defend itself because Hamas would decapitate the Palestinian Authority, Islamic extremists would flow into the West Bank, and a jihadist regime would establish fortifications on the hills overlooking the greater Tel Aviv municipal area.

Yet both left and right are also wrong, Goodman insisted, by virtue of their inability to recognize the truth in the other's claims. The way out of the trap, he counsels, is to take seriously both the demographic threat and the security threat.

The spirit of "all or nothing," according to Goodman, also ensnares Israeli thinking about religion and secularism. An observant Jew and a grateful student of secular Zionism, he lives the conflict his new book describes.

An insider in both camps, and therefore simultaneously a perpetual outsider, Goodman provides a sympathetic distillation of each side's arguments. That sets the stage for an account of how, by remaining true to themselves, the antagonists can become allies. Weaving together traditional Jewish sources, classical philosophical texts, ideas developed by the intellectual founding fathers of Zionism, social science, and contemporary cultural criticism, Goodman fashions a middle way that eases but does not overcome—indeed, it rejects as fanciful the ambition to overcome—the conflict between religion and secularism.

According to the classic critique of religion, which blossomed during the Enlightenment but stretches back to Lucretius, faith "cultivates hatred, blindness, and violence." A more nuanced critique of Orthodox Judaism, Goodman observes, blames it for fostering a sense of guilt stemming from the experience of always falling short of God's commandments, coupled with a censoriousness toward others who similarly prove ill-equipped to meet divine demands. Orthodox Judaism also sacrifices intellectual integrity when it calls on believers to reject science and history where they conflict with faith. And it betrays the moral conscience insofar as it denies basic tenets of modern freedom and equality, such as the obligation to ensure that all occupations and opportunities are in principle open to women.

Secularism also has been subject to a radical critique and a more nuanced one. The former, according to Goodman, declares that the atrocities perpetrated on an unprecedented scale in the twentieth century in the name of Nazism and Communism have roots in enlightened Europe's repudiation of sacred restraints. The latter, he explains, holds secularism responsible for generating a hubristic and emaciated individualism that has weakened families, eroded the associations of civil society, and created a society of lonely, isolated, and narcissistic people. Draining the world of transcendent principles and enduring duties, secularism has left humanity more exposed and vulnerable to the enervating lures of consumerism, the entertainment industry, and social media.

Goodman believes that secularists are correct that Orthodox Judaism betrays a tendency to inculcate a demeaning obedience to inherited authority and that Orthodox Jews are correct that secularism often fans the flames of reckless rebellion against authority of all sorts. But both are also wrong, he argues, insofar as they equate the excesses of the other with its essence.

In a wonderful reconstruction of generally neglected intellectual resources within secular Zionism and within the Orthodox Judaism of Israel's Mizrachi—that is, Middle Eastern—Jews, Goodman shows that not only the critics but also, in many cases, the defenders of secularism and religion overlook the dialogue that both sides authorize and even require.

The secular emphasis on human freedom, Goodman argues, can inspire nonbelievers to break from the prejudice that religion only diminishes individuals and communities and never enriches and elevates them. It can also emancipate those who reject God to consider afresh, without embracing faith, venerable teachings about family, community, and tradition that the secular world has obscured but the religious world has preserved.

At the same time, the biblical teaching that human beings are created in God's image and thus endowed with an innate dignity should open believers' eyes, without diminishing their religious devotion, to the variety of ways of being human. This variety includes the individual freedom, equality before the law, and celebration of each person's unique gifts that secularism at its best cherishes.

Perhaps Goodman understates the enduring tension between religion and secularism. Orthodox Judaism declares God and his law the highest authority, while secularism typically recognizes no higher authorities than human reason and will. Accordingly, the more a secular Jew immerses himself or herself in Judaism's sacred texts and traditional practices, the more he or she confronts the steadfast claims of divine revelation. And the more a religious Jew examines secular writings, culture, and daily life, the more he or she encounters the resolute affirmation of human sovereignty.

It might be more accurate to say, however, that Goodman turns the tension between religion and secularism to the advantage of both by focusing on the truths that they can teach each other while acknowledging that a perfect reconciliation is bound to elude us.

By fostering toleration and mutual understanding, recovering "another secularism" and "another religiosity" may have the additional benefit—in the United States as in Israel—of tempering the increasingly entrenched enmity between right and left.

14

BOLSTERING THE ABRAHAM ACCORDS THROUGH EDUCATION INITIATIVES

March 21, 2021

Last September energetic Trump-administration diplomacy brought Bahrain's foreign minister, the United Arab Emirates' foreign minister, and Israel's prime minister to the White House to sign and to celebrate the Abraham Accords. The agreements offer unprecedented opportunities for the parties to the accords, for the broader region, and for the international order. Over the last seven months, the focus understandably has been on cooperation in national security and commerce. More attention now should be given to education initiatives, which can serve the shared interests of Abraham Accord nations by opening minds and hearts, promoting mutual understanding, and forging the lasting bonds that are among the long-term benefits reaped by those who learn together.

The Abraham Accords are not the first agreements to establish normal relations between Israel and Arab countries. The 1979 peace treaty between Israel and Egypt brokered by President Jimmy Carter brought dramatic security gains to the Jewish state by removing the threat posed by the region's most populous country while restoring the Sinai Peninsula to Egypt. The 1994 peace treaty between Israel and Jordan, facilitated by the 1993 Oslo Accords signed by Israel and the Palestinian Liberation Organization at a White House ceremony presided over by President Bill Clinton, formalized a long-standing working relationship between Jerusalem and Amman.

Advantageous as the 1979 and 1994 treaties have been to the signatories, the countries have not progressed beyond cold peace. While the formal agreements took war off the table, established embassies, and instituted regular diplomatic channels of communication, commerce remains limited, and tourism in both directions, especially from Egypt and Jordan to Israel, is meager.

The Abraham Accords are different. They normalized relations but did not need to end hostilities, as Israel was never at war with Bahrain and the UAE. At the same time, like the 1979 and 1994 peace treaties, the Abraham Accords are grounded in national security calculations.

Bahrain, the UAE, and Israel have long shared a vital interest in countering the Islamic Republic of Iran's funding of terrorism, pursuit of nuclear weapons, and imperial ambitions. Indeed, the Abraham Accords build on years of behind-the-scenes security cooperation. But in contrast to Israel's peace treaties with Egypt and Jordan, the agreements with Bahrain and the UAE also have unleashed a keen desire among the parties to cooperate in the commercial sphere and to visit one another's countries.

The excitement is palpable. Governments eagerly prepared for the exchange of ambassadors and brought friendly relations out into the open. Entrepreneurs rushed in to invest and strike deals. Israel and Bahrain and Israel and the UAE launched commercial air travel between their countries, and notwithstanding the pandemic, tourists leaped at the opportunity.

Educators should build on the momentum. By bringing students and scholars together, cross-cultural education initiatives do more than serve the high purposes of transmitting knowledge, encouraging the search for truth, and cultivating independent minds. They also have far-reaching ancillary effects—fostering the exchange of outlooks and experiences, enriching the appreciation of the complex interplay of tradition and common humanity in the formation of peoples and nations, and building networks of lifelong friends and colleagues.

Israel and the UAE have taken the first steps to create what should become a variety of vibrant student-exchange programs. Much more can be done. Universities should establish visiting professorships to bring Israeli scholars to teach in the Gulf, and Bahraini and Emirati scholars to teach in Israel. And they should provide financial incentives to encourage faculty members to devise proposals for academic conferences that focus on issues of special interest to all three Middle Eastern countries, as well as to the United States—from desalination and the environment to comparative religion and religious freedom.

Universities, however, are not the only source of educational initiatives. In recent years the United States has witnessed the growth of a new model rooted in and funded by the private sector. This model revolves around seminars that study classic books, supplemented by a variety of guest speakers and cultural excursions. It gathers students—for a few days, a week, a month or two—to explore big ideas with a small group of peers. Such programs encourage students to continue classroom discussions on walks, over meals, and late into the evening. Instead of disseminating a single approved set of policies or ideas, such programs create a community devoted to joint inquiry and the lively exchange of views based on shared respect for basic rights and fundamental freedoms.

Over the last decade and in the United States and Israel, I have had the good fortune to teach in several such undertakings—through the Tikvah Fund, the Hertog Foundation, the George W. Bush Presidential Center, and The Public Interest Fellowship. The model could easily be adapted for a variety of educational programs that brought together, say, 25 or so Bahrainis, Emiratis, Israelis, and Americans for intense study and leisurely conversation.

The first program might be called the Principles of Freedom Seminar. Intended for promising twentysomethings and thirtysomethings, it would draw participants from government, business, journalism, security, medicine, and the academy. It could be easily adapted to students of many ages, from high school to accomplished senior figures across professions and disciplines. Its curriculum would consist of seminal works by renowned thinkers in the tradition of modern freedom, including Locke, Montesquieu, Smith, Madison, Burke, Tocqueville, and Mill. By setting aside the political controversies of the moment and instead focusing on pivotal writings on a topic of abiding importance, such a seminar enables students to engage robustly while avoiding the divisive issues arising out of contemporary politics. At the same time, a thoughtful examination of the principles of modern freedom is bound to illuminate controversies that students encounter in their own countries.

The second program could be named the Common Traditions Seminars (an approach developed by my friend and former US State Department Policy Planning Staff colleague Andrew Doran). It, too, could be designed for students of quite different ages. Its point of departure is that Jews, Christians, and Muslims share a common biblical heritage and that great philosophers in all three traditions undertook enduring efforts in the Middle Ages to reconcile their faiths with the wisdom of Plato and Aristotle. The first half of the seminar would concentrate on biblical passages of surpassing importance to the three Abrahamic religions. The second half would explore influential arguments from the outstanding medieval philosopher of each of the traditions: al-Farabi, Maimonides, and Thomas Aquinas.

The third program might be titled the Law, Nation, and Faith Seminar. It would bring reporters, columnists, editorial writers, and editors together to undertake an in-depth study of a select aspect of one of the large forces influencing regional politics. Journalists from the four countries would enhance one another's appreciation of the issues by sharing their experiences and perspectives on matters of common concern. They would return home with ideas for stories, unexpected angles on familiar controversies, and a host of new contacts, sources, and colleagues.

These three seminars, and variations that could follow on their heels, needn't remain restricted to original Abraham Accords signatories. As soon as is practically possible, citizens from Sudan, Kosovo, and Morocco—countries that all recently normalized relations with Israel—should be invited to join. The same goes for Jordanians, Egyptians, and Palestinians. And why not reach out to the Republic of Cyprus, a vibrant democracy in the eastern Mediterranean eager to contribute to regional stability and prosperity?

Of surpassing inherent value, education can play a vital role along with the advancement of shared interests in security and commerce in bolstering the Abraham Accords.

15

THE CONSERVATIVE PUZZLE IN ISRAEL

August 7, 2022, discussing "The Right Has an Opportunity to Formulate a Clear Agenda. It Should Take Advantage of It" by Gadi Taub

Israelis on the right have discovered conservatism's rich intellectual tradition. Of special interest to them, especially among the religious Zionists at the forefront of the expanding effort to develop a distinctively Israeli conservatism, is American conservatism's relation to their fledgling movement. The transnational appeal of US-style conservatism should be of special interest to Americans as well.

A few weeks ago, Ben Shapiro, the outspoken and acerbic American conservative commentator and Orthodox Jew, addressed an enthusiastic Tel Aviv crowd at a Conservative Political Action Conference event, part of CPAC's efforts to develop ties with conservatives abroad. Shapiro told the thousands in attendance that Israel could count on reliable support in the United States only from the Orthodox among Jews and the Republicans among America's two dominant political parties. Reporting on the event, *Israel Hayom* journalist Ariel Kahana cautioned against uncritical acceptance of Shapiro's counsel. In the United States, he noted, many non-Orthodox Jews, independents, and Democrats also back Israel, and Republicans don't always control the White House and Congress.

Kahana is right. As they turn to American ideas and experience to refine their views, members of the Israeli conservative movement would do well to recognize not only the intricacies of US politics but also the complexities of American conservatism.

These complexities spring from the blending of the several traditions that formed the United States. The numerous Protestant sects to which most Americans belonged in the Founding Era tended to agree that toleration and the separation of church and state reflect both God's will and the imperatives of reason. The educated class in eighteenth-century America also embraced the classical Roman ideal of a public-spirited citizenry that maintains freedom by exercising civic virtue. And most Americans at the time of the country's founding took as axiomatic the view—elaborated by seventeenth-century British thinker John Locke and affirmed in 1776 by Thomas Jefferson in the Declaration of Independence—that human beings are by nature free and equal and that the principal purpose of government is to secure unalienable rights shared equally by all.

This founding inheritance reverberates throughout American history. It was instrumental in enabling the United States to overcome the evil of slavery, vindicate the fundamental rights of women and other classes of citizens who have been wrongly denied the equal protection of the laws, and build a prosperous, democratic superpower composed of citizens from every region of the world.

In a feature in last weekend's supplement to the Hebrew-language daily newspaper *Haaretz*, titled "The Right Has an Opportunity to Formulate a Clear Agenda. It Should Take Advantage of It," my friend Gadi Taub argues that Israeli conservatives must appreciate better not only the complexities of conservatism in America but also the complexities of the conservative challenge in Israel. He is suited to make the case.

A leading conservative voice in Israel, Taub holds a PhD in American history from Rutgers University and is a senior lecturer in the School of

Public Policy and the Department of Communications at the Hebrew University of Jerusalem. He is also a *Haaretz* columnist and a podcast host; a scholar and a polemicist; well versed in America and deeply rooted in Israel; a respecter of tradition and a lover of freedom; an accomplished and well-traveled intellectual; a defender of ordinary people, local communities, and national traditions; and a lifelong Zionist who, over the course of the last two decades, has migrated from the left to the right. Taub is keenly attuned to the layers of paradox that mark the effort to transplant American conservatism in Israel.

In his lengthy essay, Taub emphasizes that American conservatism itself is marked by "internal contradictions." The most basic, he argues, is between America's classical liberal heritage and the seminal critique of abstract rights and individual choice in the name of tradition, knowledge grounded in experience, and gradual reform championed by eighteenth-century British statesman Edmund Burke, the founding father of modern conservatism. But, Taub observes—citing the 2020 report of the US State Department's Commission on Unalienable Rights, for which I served as executive secretary—individual rights and limited government are woven into the very fabric of America's traditions. Consequently, in the United States, preserving freedom is essential to the conservative task.

Preserving freedom, however, can't be the entirety of the conservative task, Taub hastens to add. That's because freedom, as the Commission on Unalienable Rights report also stresses, is neither self-sustaining nor the comprehensive good and the last word about justice. Freedom, for example, depends on citizens' character. And while carving out room for individual choice, freedom does not determine which choices and attachments best promote flourishing lives.

Accordingly, American conservatives also undertake to encourage the virtues on which freedom and flourishing depend and to counteract excesses to which the individualism that freedom fosters gives rise. Instead of relying principally on government to fortify freedom and mitigate its disadvantages, American conservatives seek to safeguard other essential features of the American tradition that restrain wayward impulses, teach duties, and bolster community and political cohesiveness. Foremost among these for American conservatives are family, faith, and nation.

In clarifying their core principles, Taub advises, Israeli conservatives should neither get lost in such policy debates as gun rights and abortion that currently preoccupy American conservatives, nor should they expect definitive answers to the controversies that roil Israeli politics. For the moment they should focus on the larger question concerning the character of their movement: Is the American synthesis of Locke and Burke—the balancing of freedom and tradition—appropriate for an Israeli conservatism?

One obstacle, Taub observes, is the socialism bound up with Israel's founding ethos and which exerts influence throughout the Israeli political spectrum. That cuts against the easy implantation into the Israeli body politic of an American conservatism for which free-market principles are a central component.

Yet Taub argues that a commitment to free-market ideas, spurred by four decades of government reform, has taken root in Israel. Today free-market beliefs are found where one might expect—among wealthy, predominantly secular high-tech elites who are in large measure Ashkenazi Jews whose ancestry is European. But capitalism has also been embraced by Mizrachi Jews of North African and Middle Eastern descent. Many are working class, vote for Likud Party leader and former Prime Minister Benjamin Netanyahu, and see themselves as scorned by Israel's progressive elites.

Israel's sizable population of Mizrachi Jews, Taub argues, must form the backbone of any organic and viable conservative movement in Israel. Indeed, many among the Mizrachi community are known as "traditionalists" because of their propensity to cherish family, faith, and the nation. In contrast to progressive elites, who tend to believe that Zionism and Jewish faith are incompatible, Mizrachi traditionalists typically see a smooth fit between Jewish nationalism and Jewish belief.

Moreover, having suffered discrimination, particularly in the 1950s, 1960s, and 1970s, at the hands of Israel's then-semisocialist Ashkenazi establishment, Mizrachi Jews played a major role in the mid-'70s in ending the control over government enjoyed by the Israeli left since the country's 1948 founding. In 1977 large numbers of the Mizrachi community embraced Menachem Begin's mix of classical liberalism and Zionism, which propelled the Likud Party leader to the prime ministership. That mix also has served Netanyahu well.

Over the decades the combination of nationalism and freedom, according to Taub, "not only promised, but operated to open paths to, mobility." Since the mid-1990s, Israel's GDP per capita has increased by more than 50 percent, and the income gap between Ashkenazi and Mizrachi has steadily decreased. As a result, writes Taub, "Milton Friedman was integrated into the Likud, and the liberal-national synthesis was established as a fundamental principle among its traditionalist voters."

To make good on their aspiration to develop a self-conscious Israeli conservatism, maintains Taub, religious Zionist intellectuals must grasp that the Mizrachi traditionalists represent the "wide and sturdy base of that which deserves to be called conservatism in Israel." Beyond publications and conferences, according to Taub, it is vital for conservative intellectuals in Israel to form a coalition with the traditionalist voters who live their conservatism without need of lectures, seminars, and learned writings.

In this Taub provides further confirmation of Burke's pertinence to Israeli conservatism. Like his heirs in the post–World War II conservative movement in America, Burke defended the moral outlook and everyday ways of ordinary people from the pretensions of those keen to use government to dictate morals and manage citizens' lives.

Taub also confirms the importance to Israeli conservatism of Locke and liberal democracy. Democracy, he stresses, enables the people to give political expression to their culture and national identity. Taub does not stress it, but individual freedom—basic civil and political liberties of the sort that flow from unalienable rights—is also essential in a pluralistic democracy like Israel's. By limiting state power, individual rights both safeguard minorities from oppressive expressions of majority will and protect the majority from managerial elites, judges, and government bureaucrats determined on their own authority to override majority preferences and moral judgments to implement their class's preferences and moral judgments. Individual rights and the respect for human dignity that they reflect, moreover, have strong roots in Zionism, as attested to by the appeals to basic rights and fundamental freedoms in Israel's Declaration of Independence.

Well understood, carefully translated, and prudently applied, American conservatism's synthesis of Locke and Burke nourishes distinctively Israeli conservatism.

16

ISRAEL PUTS NETANYAHU'S CONSERVATIVE ZIONISM TO THE TEST

November 27, 2022

TEL AVIV—After five elections in three and a half years, former Israeli Prime Minister Benjamin Netanyahu has assembled a substantial coalition. On November 1 Netanyahu's Likud garnered 32 seats, making it the largest party by far in the 120-member Knesset. Voters gave his bloc, the most right-wing in Israel's history, a relatively comfortable 64 seats. Negotiations with coalition members could lead to the swearing in of a new government any day now. The question is whether Netanyahu, loved by many on the right and loathed by many in the center and on the left, will provide Israel the security, stability, and prosperity that he promises or will prove poison, as his detractors firmly believe, to a troubled body politic.

Netanyahu ran hard to the right. He galvanized his base while buttressing his support with ultranationalists seeking to maintain Israeli control over Judea and Samaria and ultra-Orthodox keen to retain their exemptions from military service and sizable state subsidies for their religious schools.

On a few noteworthy occasions since the election, Netanyahu has moderated his tone. Late at night after the polls closed on November 1, even as he proclaimed to a boisterous crowd that he would create a stable right-wing government, he offered conciliatory remarks: "I intend to be prime minister of all citizens of Israel, Jews and non-Jews alike. I care about everybody." On November 13, after formally receiving the mandate to form a government from Israeli President Isaac Herzog, Netanyahu reiterated his unifying intentions: "I intend to be a prime minister for everyone—for those who voted for me, and for those who did not vote for me."

For veteran *New York Times* columnist Thomas Friedman, Netanyahu's mollifying words count for nothing. Three days after the election in "The Israel We Knew Is Gone," Friedman pronounced anathema on Netanyahu and his coalition. Touting his 40 years covering the Middle East, but regurgitating progressive conventional wisdom, Friedman decried the incoming Netanyahu government as a "nightmare" and a "previously unthinkable reality." Among the members of Netanyahu's coalition, Friedman singled out Itamar Ben-Gvir, a leader of the Jewish Power Party, and Bezalel Smotrich, head of the Religious Zionist Party. The former "was convicted by an Israeli court in 2007 of incitement to racism and supporting a Jewish terrorist organization." The latter "has long advocated outright Israeli annexation of the West Bank and argued that there is 'no such thing as Jewish terrorism' when it comes to settlers retaliating on their own against Palestinian violence."

Friedman's apocalyptic pronouncements spring from understandable apprehensions, but he too hastily concludes that Netanyahu is bound to acquiesce to his coalition partners' worst excesses. For cooler heads and more incisive analysis, it is useful to turn to the Hebrew-language newspaper *Makor Rishon.*

Affiliated with religious Zionism and right-wing nationalism, *Makor Rishon* has, since Netanyahu's victory, published two excellent assessments of his signal achievements, his costly shortcomings, and the fateful crossroads at which he now stands. On November 11 weekly columnist Ari Shavit, best-selling author of *My Promised Land: The Triumph and Tragedy of Israel*, illuminated key chapters in Netanyahu's previous turns at prime minister. In a long feature published the day before—a review of Netanyahu's recently released memoir, *Bibi: My Story*—Micah Goodman, best-selling author of *Catch-67: The Ideas Behind the Controversy That Is Tearing Israel Apart*, examined the ideas that have dominated Netanyahu's thinking about Zionism and Israel since his youth. Shavit and Goodman display the rare ability to write about both right and left in Israel with sympathy and understanding while also drawing conclusions and reaching judgments. Their postelection commentary throws into sharp relief Netanyahu's great opportunity, as well as the snares and delusions that he must overcome to govern Israel responsibly.

In "The Big Question: Who Will Be the Fourth Netanyahu?," Shavit identifies the first Netanyahu as Israel's prime minister from 1996 to 1999. The young, ambitious "national-pragmatic leader" accepted the 1993 Oslo Accords, which established the Palestinian Authority, returned Yasser Arafat in 1994 as the PA's first president, and promised Israel's gradual withdrawal from Judea and Samaria and the Gaza Strip. However, Netanyahu "slowed considerably the process of withdrawal, reduced terrorism, and stabilized Israel."

The second Netanyahu regained the prime minister's office in 2009 and endured for six years. He cunningly created a military option to attack Tehran's nuclear program, Shavit argues, the real purpose of which was to impel then-President Obama to take a tougher stance toward Tehran. The plan partially worked, buying Israel time. Although the United States adopted strong sanctions against Iran and imposed a "political-economic blockade," President Obama's 2015 Iran deal was a "terrible missed opportunity."

The third Netanyahu emerged in 2015. "The tumultuous victory in the 2015 election, the criminal investigations opened against him shortly after, and the rise of Donald Trump fundamentally changed Bibi," writes Shavit.

"Persecuted and monarchical," Netanyahu "abandoned the pragmatic nationalism and shed the patrician elegance" that had characterized him since he entered Israeli politics. The criminal investigations issued in indictments in 2019 and then, in 2020, trial for bribery, fraud, and breach of trust. He remained in power through three inconclusive elections, beginning in April 2019 and continuing until spring 2021, when he was unseated in a fourth election by a coalition led by conservative Naftali Bennett and centrist Yair Lapid, which included left-wing parties and an Arab party. While signing in 2020 the historic Abraham Accords, "the recent years of his government have been wrapped in flames of faction, invective, and brotherly hatred."

Shavit does not pretend to know who will emerge as the fourth Netanyahu. The once and future prime minister will want to focus on the Iran challenge, which requires progress in normalizing relations with Saudi Arabia, and on the economy. But given the incoming government's dependence on ultranationalists and the ultra-Orthodox, who demand dramatic changes, along with the burdens of defending himself in court, Shavit wonders whether Netanyahu can "unite anew a divided and quarrelsome people."

Netanyahu can't rely on the center and left, which lie in tatters because of his decisive electoral victory, to provide balance, restraint, and moderation. "Now, Netanyahu's only balancer, restrainer, and moderator is Netanyahu himself," writes Shavit. "He will decide how history will judge the fourth—and final—Netanyahu."

The same Netanyahu who has repeatedly resorted to vulgar demagoguery and has presided over growing factionalism, maintains Goodman in "The Paradox of Netanyahu," also has consistently exercised a distinctive form of moderation. A "double caution"—toward conducting peace negotiations and toward deploying the army—marks the career of Israel's longest-serving prime minister, Goodman observes. "His critics were not always aware that Netanyahu's double caution is not a sacrifice of his beliefs but rather their full realization."

A brand of political realism, Goodman shows, circumscribes Netanyahu's Zionism. For Bibi, "the sole guarantee of the continuation of the Jewish people is the transformation of Israel into a state possessing exceptional abilities and powers," Goodman writes. "And this is Netanyahu's formula for building Israeli power: Economic success will enable the building of military capabilities and the mixture of economic and military power will in turn produce political and diplomatic power."

Other forms of Zionism have pursued lofty goals. Left-wing secular Zionists envisage Israel as a model socialist society. Right-wing religious Zionists dream of a state that reflects the Jewish spirit and honors Jewish law. In contrast, Goodman maintains, Netanyahu regards Israel's goal as the state of Israel itself. According to Netanyahu's Zionism, the state's overriding purpose is to assure the Jewish people's survival in a dangerous world that is, and always has been, especially dangerous for the Jewish people.

The paradox, according to Goodman, is that while no one has contributed more to polarization in Israel than Netanyahu, no one has given more effective expression to the "hidden agreement" that has crystallized among Israelis that the state exists to provide security against the hostile forces arrayed against the Jews.

Netanyahu's thinking is, Goodman asserts, "conservative in the most literal sense of the word." That's correct inasmuch as self-preservation is the prerequisite to every other human experience and achievement. Yet accepting Netanyahu's sober conviction that after the establishment of the state of Israel, Zionism's proper aim is to preserve the nation, the inspiring fact remains that Israel, as its Declaration of Independence affirms, is constituted in part by commitment to a Jewish state that secures freedom, justice, peace, and the rights shared by all its citizens.

To preserve the nation, Netanyahu must conserve the full range of principles on which Israel is based. That is crucial to fostering across the Jewish state's many factions and fault lines the political cohesiveness essential to the security, stability, and prosperity that he promises.

17

FORMER ISRAELI COMMANDERS SAY SEPARATE FROM PALESTINIANS

December 30, 2022

TEL AVIV—On December 29 Benjamin Netanyahu was sworn in for the sixth time as Israel's prime minister. As in each of his previous terms, the nation confronts substantial national security challenges. Although little mentioned during the run-up to the November 1 election, the Israeli-Palestinian conflict remains among them.

That's because Israel is a rights-protecting democracy. Harsh security realities and intense nationalist and religious convictions also surround the question of the ultimate disposition of the disputed territories known here both as the West Bank (more common on the left) and Judea and Samaria (typical of the right). The land, which forms the heart of biblical Israel, also is home to approximately 2.75 million Palestinians (not to be confused with Israel's roughly 2 million Arab citizens). The Jewish state, however, cannot indefinitely exercise authority over another people against their will and remain true to its free and democratic principles.

In 1996, when Netanyahu assembled his first government, the struggle over the disputed territories was front and center. A wave of Palestinian suicide-bombing attacks terrorized the country. The grisly violence against Israel's civilian population took place against the background of the 1995 assassination of Prime Minister Yitzhak Rabin by an Israeli religious ultranationalist who, following the 1993 Oslo Accords, sought to save Israel from further compromises with the Palestinians.

A quarter of a century later, voters gave little heed to the conflict, yet the stakes remain high. Whereas in 2005 Prime Minister Ariel Sharon withdrew all Israeli forces and the entire Israeli civilian population from the Gaza Strip, the number of Israelis living in the West Bank has more than doubled in the intervening 18 years, jumping from around 225,000 to approximately 475,000.

Several factors contribute to Israelis' declining interest over the last two decades in the Israeli-Palestinian conflict. None diminishes the conflict's long-term significance.

First, the Palestinian issue has worn down Israelis. The last four US presidents—Clinton, Bush, Obama, and Trump—sought to broker peace accords, to no avail.

Second, Israel suffers from deep cleavages. Teeming with triumphalism, the right believes that its 64-seat majority in Israel's 120-member Knesset confers a mandate to implement far-reaching changes in the legal system, education, and state funding of the ultra-Orthodox. Meanwhile, outgoing Prime Minister Yair Lapid labeled Netanyahu's new government "dangerous, extreme, irresponsible," while accomplished Tel Aviv professionals in their fifties and sixties mourn the loss of their country and speak grimly of taking to the streets.

Third, despite the failure to make headway with the Palestinians, Israelis have, since the dissipation of the Second Intifada in the mid-2000s, enjoyed a robust economy. Free-market reforms introduced in the early 2000s by then-Minister of the Treasury Netanyahu helped unleash the nation's entrepreneurial spirit, creating opportunities for young Israelis to commercialize high-tech prowess developed during mandatory military service and producing unprecedented affluence.

Fourth, by the late 1990s, the Israeli national security establishment had concluded that the Islamic Republic of Iran's nuclear program represented the paramount danger. No one has done more to educate Israelis and the world about the Iran threat than Netanyahu. Nevertheless, Tehran stands on the threshold of producing nuclear weapons. And with a tailwind from their $400 billion trade deal with China in 2021, Iran's ayatollahs persist in sowing terror throughout the region, not least on Israel's borders, by backing Hezbollah in Lebanon, Hamas in Gaza and the West Bank, and Syrian dictator Bashar al-Assad.

Fifth, the Trump administration–brokered Abraham Accords have yielded considerable fruit and offer hope of greater cooperation between Israel, the Gulf Arabs, and the wider Muslim world. Expanding commercial relations in the Gulf have the potential to create millions of jobs in the region and produce hundreds of billions of dollars of economic activity. Israel, moreover, has signed security cooperation agreements with Bahrain and Morocco and in 2021 conducted a joint naval exercise in the Red Sea with Bahrain, the United Arab Emirates, and the United States. Speculation swirls about drawing the Saudis into the accords, but based on Riyadh's public statements, that will require Israel to show tangible progress regarding the Palestinians.

The trouble is that because of the multifarious developments that have deflected their attention from the conflict, many Israelis have effectively embraced Netanyahu's unofficial approach, at least since he reclaimed the prime ministership in 2009: muddle through, buy time, kick the can down the road. Soon after his return to power, and where consistent with Israeli security, Netanyahu adopted measures to strengthen the Palestinian economy. More recently, he has given Israelis who favor annexation of parts or all of Judea and Samaria reason to believe he is on their side while taking no formal actions that preclude the establishment of a Palestinian state in the West Bank.

But circumstances don't stand still. The number of Israelis living in Judea and Samaria grows while violence there rises.[1] The pro-Western Kingdom of Jordan, which is vital to US and Israeli regional interests, displays mounting hostility to Israel over lack of progress on the Palestinian question.[2] The sclerotic and kleptocratic Palestinian Authority has made Hamas, which has ruled the Gaza Strip since 2007, a popular alternative in the West Bank. At the same time, younger Palestinians living in Judea and Samaria, despairing of attaining a state of their own, increasingly aspire to full citizenship in Israel, which would change Israel from a Jewish state to a binational state.

In the face of mounting volatility, Commanders for Israel's Security (CIS) maintains that Israel's informal policy of having no policy in Judea and Samaria must end. Security imperatives for the preservation of Israel as a Jewish, free, and democratic state, the organization argues, require prompt action to reduce Israeli responsibility for governing West Bank Palestinians.

A nonpartisan organization founded in 2014, CIS's more than 400 members include retired senior officials of Israel's defense establishment—the military (Israel Defense Forces), the national intelligence agency (Mossad), internal security (Shabak), and the Israel Police—as well as of Israel's diplomatic corps. The retired officials "are united in the conviction that a two-state agreement with the Palestinians, as part of a regional security framework, is essential for Israel's security as well as for its future as the democratic home of the Jewish People." But CIS recognizes that "current conditions are not conducive" to attaining a two-state agreement.

---

1 Emanuel Fabian, "2022 among the Deadliest Years in Recent Memory for Israelis and Palestinians," *Times of Israel,* December 13, 2022, https://www.timesofisrael.com/2022-shaping-up-to-be-deadliest-for-israelis-and-palestinians-in-years.

2 Jonathan Schanzer, "Neither Here nor There: Jordan and the Abraham Accords," Foundation for Defense of Democracies, December 8, 2022, https://www.fdd.org/wp-content/uploads/2022/12/fdd-memo-neither-here-nor-there-jordan-and-the-abraham-accords.pdf.

Over the short term, therefore, CIS recommends "civilian separation" of Israel from West Bank Palestinians with the IDF maintaining responsibility for security in the territories. This pragmatic approach, the former commanders believe, can preserve the conditions that eventually would allow for the emergence of a Palestinian state. At the same time, many of the immediate steps they propose to ease the conflict are consistent with the annexation of, say, Israel's major West Bank settlement blocs, which are home to a substantial majority of the Israelis in Judea and Samaria. Accordingly, the CIS aspiration "to forge a broad national consensus" fits with key overlapping goals of Israel's substantial bloc of center-left and center-right voters.

Published in November 2021, CIS's "Initiative 2025: Immediate Term Actions to Promote Israel's Security" elaborates a mix of security and developmental measures to advance civilian separation. For example, CIS urges Israel to finish building the security barrier that was begun in 2002 in response to the Second Intifada, of which approximately 390 of the planned 462 miles have been completed. The CIS plan also calls for constructing more dedicated roads in Judea and Samaria for Palestinian traffic. These undertakings would reduce friction with Israeli forces and civilians, increase contiguity among the 186 Palestinian-controlled districts that form areas A and B under the Oslo Accords, strengthen PA governance, and boost PA prosperity.

In addition, the CIS plan recommends increasing the number of permits for West Bank Palestinians to work in Israel. It also advises Israel to ease restrictions on Palestinian goods, both within the West Bank and for export; spur Palestinian trade by removing financial restrictions and red tape; and assist in constructing Palestinian industrial zones and improving Palestinian agriculture.

Separation does not mean severing relations with the Palestinians. On the contrary, CIS Director Itamar Yaar told me that the achievement of civilian separation will depend on extensive cooperation between the two peoples living between the Jordan River and the Mediterranean Sea.

Relying on ultranationalist and ultra-Orthodox parties, Netanyahu's coalition government leaves Israel's longest-serving prime minister limited room to maneuver on the Israeli-Palestinian conflict. Yet civilian separation from the West Bank Palestinians fits well with his conservative Zionism, which, like CIS, seeks to preserve Israel as a free, democratic, and Jewish state.

Securing his legacy—and Israel's long-term national security—will demand an adroitness from Netanyahu that will test the limits of his acclaimed political skills.

18

ISRAEL'S CONSTITUTIONAL COUNTERREVOLUTION

February 5, 2023

In the 1990s then-Israeli Supreme Court President Aharon Barak led a constitutional revolution, arrogating to the judiciary virtually unchecked power to rule on an expansive array of public issues. Today Prime Minister Benjamin Netanyahu's new coalition government is advancing proposals that promise to undo Barak's constitutional revolution. Even as Knesset Constitution, Law and Justice Committee Chair Simcha Rothman has been conducting hearings to debate the proposed reforms, the Israeli left and center have decried the end of democracy in Israel, taken to the streets in the tens of thousands to protest, and threatened civil disobedience.

Yet as journalist Ben-Dror Yemini, who is not a conservative but speaks for those across the political spectrum committed to the rule of law and the separation of powers, argued last month in the Israeli daily *Yedioth Ahronoth*, reform of Israel's judiciary is necessary and long overdue. The proper scope and pace of reform, however, are open to debate and must be carefully calibrated. Accordingly, the conservative-led constitutional counterrevolution presents challenges for the burgeoning conservative movement in Israel—and for the nation.

Two stand out.

The first challenge consists in exercising prudence, which Edmund Burke celebrated as "the god of this lower world." The virtue is acquired through experience. It enhances appreciation of the complexity of circumstances, the inevitability of unintended consequences, and the wisdom embodied in inherited beliefs, practices, and institutions. It is exercised in the incremental reform of existing arrangements to meet the demands of new developments. Prudence combines judgment and execution but does not involve a method or formula. It shines in the harmonization of competing considerations and balancing of multiple principles. The pressing need to fix flawed political institutions inflects prudence but does not suspend it.

A second challenge concerns democracy, the survival of which in the Jewish state, according to both left and right in Israel, is at stake in the struggle over the legal system. Conservatives contend that especially since Israel lacks a written constitution, judicial review—the judiciary's power to strike down legislation and disallow administrative actions on the grounds that they conflict with Israel's quasi-constitutional Basic Laws or simply because they are unreasonable—must be severely circumscribed to ensure that Supreme Court justices do not substitute their preferences for the people's will expressed by their elected representatives. Meanwhile, the left maintains that the court's expansive powers must be preserved to safeguard what Justice Barak called "substantive democracy," by which he meant a host of unwritten rights and rule-of-law principles that justify restricting momentary expressions of the people's will to safeguard their long-term interests and fundamental rights.

Both sides' appeals to democracy occlude the Jewish state's composite character as a specific form of democracy—a rights-protecting or liberal democracy. Like America's 1776 Declaration of Independence, Israel's 1948 Declaration of Independence puts a premium on freedom and individual rights. Although neither mentions the word "democracy," America's declaration grounds just political power in the consent of the governed, while Israel's declaration emphasizes the "full and equal citizenship" of all the country's inhabitants "and due representation in all its provisional and permanent institutions." Both countries seek to fashion institutions that facilitate the expression of the people's will while protecting individual rights, which entails setting limits on the people's will.

Conservative friends of Israel have leapt to the Netanyahu government's defense in the face of a barrage of apocalyptic criticism. But they have tended to neglect the imperatives of prudence in devising judicial reforms that harmonize democracy and freedom in the Jewish state.

For example, with characteristic vigor and vituperation, *Newsweek* opinion editor Josh Hammer compares critics of the Netanyahu government's legal reforms to "a dog returning to its own vomit" and dismisses doubts about the constitutional counterrevolution as "performative shrieks of hysteria." Among the government's prominent critics are retired Lieutenant General Ehud Barak, Israel's tenth prime minister and former defense minister under Netanyahu; retired Lieutenant General Moshe "Bogie" Ya'alon, who also served as defense minister under Netanyahu; and retired Lieutenant General Gadi Eizenkot, who served as Israel Defense Forces chief of general staff under Netanyahu. The decorated officers have a combined total of 114 years of military service. Barak's denunciation of the government as "legal, but clearly illegitimate"[1] is reckless, but the generals' grave concerns, shared by many Israelis, should not be reduced to howling for attention.

In the *Wall Street Journal*, Eugene Kontorovich calmly enumerates several elements of the high court's original 1990s "power grab" while similarly concluding that opposition to the government's pursuit of far-reaching revisions to the relationship between the court and the

1 "Ehud Barak Says Netanyahu's Government Is Legal but 'Illegitimate,'" *Times of Israel*, January 14, 2023, https://www.timesofisrael.com/liveblog_entry/ehud-barak-says-netanyahus-government-is-legal-but-illegitimate.

legislature is without merit. A professor at George Mason University's Scalia School of Law and a fellow at the Kohelet Policy Forum in Israel, Kontorovich stresses, for instance, that the government's proposal to "increase the Knesset's involvement in judicial appointments" would fall "far short of America's purely political appointment process." He doesn't mention that the division of labor between the US president and Senate in the judicial appointment process, which often requires the cooperation of both major parties, imposes constraints absent from the government's proposal.

Kontorovich also maintains that the proposed "override clause," which would give a bare majority of 61 of the 120-member Knesset the power to invalidate judicial decisions, "would be less effective than proponents and critics think." Since the legislative process in Israel grinds slowly, he argues, the Knesset could overturn only a few of the thousands of annual Supreme Court decisions. That's true but beside the point. It's just those few especially controversial and significant cases—involving, say, the rights of dissenters and of individuals who belong to unpopular groups, or conflicts of interest among members of the government—where the checks and balances provided by an independent judiciary are most needed.

Writing for *Commentary*, Elliott Abrams refrains from taking a stand on the judicial reforms, but his explanation of American Jews' "hysterical reaction" to the new Netanyahu government obscures a crucial dimension of the controversy in Israel. Chairman of the Tikvah Fund and a board member of the Jewish People Policy Institute and the Israeli Democracy Institute, Abrams is a seasoned and shrewd observer of Israeli politics and the American Jewish community. One source of American Jewish hysteria, he suggests, is simple ignorance of the reasons Israelis have for viewing the court as "deeply undemocratic and imperious."

But the deeper problem, Abrams contends, is that as American Jews grow more secular and progressive, they become increasingly incapable of appreciating an Israel that has evolved into a conservative country that puts a premium on maintaining its Jewish character in a dangerous neighborhood. To underscore the point, Abrams quotes Robert Kagan's memorable statement from the time of the US-led 2003 invasion of Iraq: "On major strategic and international questions today, Americans are from Mars and Europeans are from Venus."

Kagan's witticism, however, misled 20 years ago and does so today in relation to American Jews and Israel. In 2003, as in 2023, plenty of Americans also were from Venus. Then as now, moreover, no small part of Europe, particularly in regions beyond the major metropolitan areas and in countries once subjugated by the Soviet dictatorship, understood, in the spirit of Mars, the harsh realities of war and conquest and the folly of supposing that bureaucrats, diplomats, and judges alone can ensure peace and prosperity.

While the vast majority of American non-Orthodox Jews may be progressives, the division between Mars and Venus, as Abrams knows, also cuts through Israel. Netanyahu's bloc obtained a solid Knesset majority of 64 seats in the November 2022 election, the fifth in four years, but received only about 30,000 more votes than the anti-Netanyahu bloc. A slender conservative majority—including the ultra-Orthodox (about 13 percent of the population) who receive enormous state subsidies while generally avoiding military service—backs the constitutional counterrevolution. Meanwhile, a large minority—much of it secular, progressive, and making vital contributions to Israel's economy and defense—opposes it. To preserve political cohesiveness, substantial changes to the structure of the Israeli regime must earn support that extends beyond these partisan divisions.

In a deft analysis of the conservative spirit in Israel, best-selling author Micah Goodman warns in the Hebrew-language newspaper *Makor Rishon* that unintended consequences flowing from the constitutional counterrevolution are likely to intensify political instability. When a center-left coalition returns to power, Goodman points out, it may well repeal, through a simple majority vote, the major changes Netanyahu's right-wing coalition seeks to enact. Or it may use the legislature's expanded powers, say, to ram through laws that impair the religious liberty of the ultra-Orthodox. Either way, in a torn nation, constitutional counterrevolution amplifies division.

Conservatives make a compelling case that balance must be restored to the separation of powers in Israel. A concern for the need to harmonize Israel's free, democratic, and Jewish character demands prudence in the pursuit of necessary constitutional reform.

19

NETANYAHU'S SAUDI ARABIA BIND

February 12, 2023

Israeli Prime Minister Benjamin Netanyahu aspires to bring Saudi Arabia into the Abraham Accords. However, he finds himself in a bind: The actions he must take to normalize relations with Riyadh conflict with the arrangements and concessions necessary to preserve his hard right-wing coalition government.

According to a statement issued by Israel's Ministry of Foreign Affairs following a mid-January meeting in Jerusalem, Netanyahu and Biden administration National Security Advisor Jake Sullivan "discussed the next steps to deepen the Abraham Accords and expand the circle of peace, with emphasis on a breakthrough regarding Saudi Arabia." In a February 1 interview with CNN's Jake Tapper, Netanyahu went further. "If we make peace with Saudi Arabia—it depends on the Saudi leadership—and bring, effectively, the Arab-Israeli conflict to an end," he said, "I think we'll circle back to the Palestinians and get a workable peace with the Palestinians."

Upgrading relations is also on the Saudi agenda but with caveats. At Davos in January, Saudi Foreign Minister Prince Faisal bin Farhan Al Saud stated that improving ties with Israel depends on progress in establishing a Palestinian state. "Palestine remains an incredibly important, evocative issue in our region," said the Saudi foreign minister. "It remains incredibly consequential and remains unresolved. And the focus really needs to be on a pathway to resolving this conflict, and that's only going to happen with negotiations between the Palestinians and the Israelis, in the spirit of reaching real agreements and reaching in the end, we believe, a Palestinian state with East Jerusalem as its capital."

Bin Farhan Al Saud acknowledged that Israel is "sending some signals that maybe are not conducive" to formal negotiations and enduring agreements. At the same time, he hoped that "in the end" the Israelis understand "it is in their interest—and not just their interest but the wider region—that they engage seriously on resolving the Palestinian conflict, because if we resolve that conflict, if we are able to find a resolution that gives the Palestinians dignity," then "that removes a huge drag on the entire region, a source of potential conflict that is always going to be there if not resolved."

The Saudi foreign minister's forward-looking remarks leave room for securing normalization without fully resolving the Israeli-Palestinian conflict. To take advantage of the opening, Israel will need to demonstrate progress in creating conditions for extending Palestinian self-government. In the CNN interview, Netanyahu sketched an approach that might fit the bill. He envisaged a "formula for peace" in which West Bank Palestinians possess "all the powers that they need to govern themselves but none of the powers that can threaten us [Israel]." In other words Israel would retain "overriding security responsibility" for the land, both that governed by Israel and that governed by the Palestinian Authority, that lies west of the Jordan River.

Two sets of concrete interests impel Israel and Saudi Arabia to pursue normalization. The first stems from shared national security concerns. In the face of the Islamic Republic of Iran's quest for hegemony in the Middle East, Riyadh and Jerusalem both recognize that they would benefit from enhanced defense cooperation. The second is a matter of economic development and commerce. Under the leadership of Crown Prince and Prime Minister Mohammed bin Salman, the kingdom has undertaken massive modernization projects for which Israel is well placed to provide high-tech know-how and sophisticated internal-security assistance.

Netanyahu has a private interest in striking a deal with Saudi Arabia. Having doubled the number of Arab countries with normal diplomatic relations with Israel by signing the historic Abraham Accords with Bahrain and the United Arab Emirates in September 2020, the country's longest-serving prime minister would cement his legacy as Israel's preeminent statesman by presiding over the exchange of ambassadors with Riyadh.

Netanyahu, however, faces a daunting challenge. In a searing essay in the *Jewish Review of Books*, the American-born author Hillel Halkin, who has lived in Israel since 1970 and who has long been associated with the conservative Zionism of Ze'ev Jabotinsky and Menachem Begin, gives reasons to doubt that the prime minister can meet the Saudis' publicly expressed preconditions for normalization. The principal impediment is that Netanyahu's religious ultranationalist coalition partners will block efforts to expand Palestinian self-rule.

Since Netanyahu returned to the prime minister's office in 2009, "not solving things but 'managing' them became the slogan of the Netanyahu governments—and the Center-Left opposition, having run out of ideas of its own, went along," observes Halkin. "The Palestinian problem, until then at the heart of Israeli political debate, was shunted aside. Nothing had worked, ergo, nothing could work; why waste time discussing it? What couldn't be solved could be lived with."

Although Israel has prospered economically over the last 14 years and notwithstanding persistent Palestinian intransigence and militancy, Halkin argues, the Palestinian problem cannot be postponed indefinitely.

What he calls the "standard formulation" of Israel's excruciating dilemma remains as true as when it emerged in the aftermath of Israel's great victory in the Six-Day War. "Unless Israel relinquished control of most of the territories acquired in 1967 along with their millions of Arab inhabitants," Halkin writes, "it would eventually have to either grant these inhabitants citizenship and cease to be a Jewish state or continue to deny it and cease to be a democratic state: a binational Israel that would inevitably implode from within or a morally repugnant Israel ostracized by the world and deserted by many of its own citizens—such would be the only, the intolerable, choice if Israel failed to extricate itself from the Palestinian quicksand."

Netanyahu grasps the issue. In the absence of negotiations that stood a chance of settling the conflict once and for all, he pursued in 2009 an "economic peace" that promoted Palestinian prosperity.[1]

In the short term, however, additional steps to ease the conflict are unlikely because of the composition of Netanyahu's 64-seat governing coalition in Israel's 120-member Knesset. In addition to his Likud Party, which won 32 seats, the coalition includes two ultra-Orthodox parties, which together hold 18 seats, and religious ultranationalist parties that control 14 seats. These partners, according to Halkin, are at best indifferent to easing the conflict.

The ultra-Orthodox parties tend to look inward. They focus on preserving their community's exemptions from military service; maintaining enormous state subsidies to their religious schools, which disdain to teach core subjects such as English and mathematics; keeping a large segment of the adult male population out of the workforce and engaged in full-time Torah study; and extending Jewish law's reach in public life.

Meanwhile, the religious ultranationalists make a priority of securing Jewish settlement in Judea and Samaria, the biblical names for the

1 Raphael Ahren, "Netanyahu: Economics, Not Politics, Is the Key to Peace," *Haaretz*, November 20, 2008, https://www.haaretz.com/2008-11-20/ty-article/netanyahu-economics-not-politics-is-the-key-to-peace/0000017f-f49d-d47e-a37f-fdbd12a10000.

territories also referred to as the West Bank. Bezalel Smotrich leads the religious ultranationalists. Under an unusual agreement with Netanyahu, Smotrich serves not only as finance minister but also as a minister in the ministry of defense. After the right's November election victory, Smotrich tweeted, according to Halkin, "With God's help, we in the incoming government will accelerate Israeli settlement in all parts of the Land of Israel."

The appeal to God as a political ally dismays Halkin. He stresses that he has long supported Israelis living in Judea and Samaria because "these were part of my people's heritage." But as a Zionist in the mold of Jabotinsky and Begin, he rejects reliance on God for the hard work of building a Jewish state that is free and democratic. Convinced that the Palestinians, too, have a legitimate claim on the disputed territories, Halkin writes, "I do not pretend to know whose side God is on, or whether he takes sides at all in such matters, or whether he still would be God if he did." Halkin's fear is that instead of shouldering responsibility to ease the conflict, Smotrich, along with the religious ultranationalists he leads and the ultra-Orthodox, has put his faith in God to handle matters on behalf of the Jewish people in God's way and on God's schedule.

Optimists argue that Smotrich and allies will grow in office and credit Netanyahu's insistence that he can control both the religious-ultranationalist and ultra-Orthodox members of his coalition. Netanyahu's legion of critics in the center and on the left contends that the prime minister—imperiled by a criminal trial on charges of bribery, fraud, and breach of trust and embroiled in controversy over a major overhaul of the judiciary—is too dependent on his coalition partners to rein them in.

One thing is for sure: Maintaining his coalition while drawing Saudi Arabia into normalization talks by taking constructive measures to promote Palestinian prosperity and self-government will require of Netanyahu political wizardry and statesmanship of an exceptionally high order.

20

THE PERTINENCE OF ISRAEL'S DECLARATION OF INDEPENDENCE

March 5, 2023, discussing Israel's Declaration of Independence: The History and Political Theory of the Nation's Founding Moment *by Neil Rogachevsky and Dov Zigler*

The outpouring of opposition in Israel to the sweeping judicial reforms advanced by Prime Minister Benjamin Netanyahu's coalition government springs from much more than disagreement about the details of the institutional mechanisms for appointing judges and the proper scope of judicial review in a rights-protecting democracy. The protests' breadth, intensity, and persistence—for the first time since the demonstrations began in January, police used stun grenades and water cannons last week against protesters who blocked major Tel Aviv arteries—reflect a fear that the government endeavors to transform the basic structure of the Israeli regime by eliminating the judiciary's independence.[1]

The fear runs deep. According to a recent poll, opponents of the government's judicial reforms, many of whom recognize the need to rein in the

1 Carrie Keller-Lynn and Emanuel Fabian, "As Protests Sweep Nation, Police Use Aggressive Means to Clear Tel Aviv Rally," *Times of Israel*, https://www.timesofisrael.com/as-protests-sweep-nation-police-use-aggressive-means-to-clear-tel-aviv-rally.

Israeli high court's expansive powers, encompass more than half the country.[2] Week after week, tens of thousands of flag-waving citizens have taken to the streets to protest what they regard as the descent of Israeli democracy into dictatorship. Upstanding members of the community—including prominent lawyers, doctors, and business executives, along with high-ranking former members of the military establishment—say that the question is not whether the country plunges into civil war but rather how the civil war into which the country has plunged will end.

The economy has been hit hard. Individuals have withdrawn savings from local banks to find safe financial havens abroad, and investors are looking to relocate their operations outside Israel.

In addition, security has been jeopardized. As of late February, more than 250 elite reservists in the special-operations division of military intelligence had signed an open letter[3]—following similar statements from reserve pilots,[4] tankists,[5] submariners,[6] and other reserve military personnel—declaring their refusal to serve if the government enacts its judicial-reform package.

Reform proponents remain determined to curb high-court judicial activism. The Israeli Supreme Court's arrogation to itself in the 1990s of far-reaching authority to invalidate legislation and dictate policy contrary

---

2 "Poll: Coalition Slumps 9 Seats, Losing Majority amid Unrest over Judicial Overhaul," *Times of Israel,* February 25, 2023, https://www.timesofisrael.com/poll-coalition-slumps-9-seats-losing-majority-amid-unrest-over-judicial-overhaul.

3 "As Reservist Rebellion Grows, IDF Chief Said Concerned It Will Harm Operations," *Times of Israel,* February 26, 2023, https://www.timesofisrael.com/as-reservist-rebellion-grows-idf-chief-said-concerned-it-will-harm-operations.

4 Emanuel Fabian, "1,000 Ex-Air Force Officers Ask Jurists to Stop New Government from Razing Democracy," *Times of Israel*, December 26, 2022, https://www.timesofisrael.com/1000-ex-air-force-officers-ask-jurists-to-stop-new-government-from-razing-democracy.

5 Emanuel Fabian, "IDF Vets End 3-Day Anti-Overhaul March with Rally, Urge PM to 'Stop This Madness,'" *Times of Israel,* February 10, 2023, https://www.timesofisrael.com/idf-vets-end-3-day-anti-overhaul-march-with-rally-urge-pm-to-stop-this-madness.

6 Judah Ari Gross, "Hundreds of Ex-Submariners Urge Stop to Overhaul 'Before We Reach the Abyss,'" *Times of Israel,* February 22, 2023, https://www.timesofisrael.com/hundreds-of-ex-submariners-urge-stop-to-overhaul-before-we-reach-the-abyss.

to majority preferences has generated enormous resentment on the right. It has also provoked incisive criticism, not least from such formidable center- and left-leaning thinkers as the late Ruth Gavison, a longtime Hebrew University professor of law.

Despite the need for reforms, opponents strenuously, even apocalyptically, reject the government's proposals because they are bound up in opponents' minds with crucial questions of religion and the state, citizenship, and the rule of law. Israelis in the center and on the left and not a few on the right see the judicial reforms as a Trojan horse intended to protect the large state subsidies received by ultra-Orthodox religious schools, as well as to safeguard the ultra-Orthodox community's exemption from military service. The critics also view the reforms as empowering those religious ultranationalists bent on applying Israeli sovereignty to the entirety of the disputed territories in Judea and Samaria. This would incorporate around 3 million Palestinians into Israel, compromising the state's Jewish character, its democratic character, or both. And they regard the reforms as enmeshing Netanyahu in a conflict of interest because the shift of power from the courts to the prime-minister-led government would give the Knesset authority to nullify unfavorable rulings in the current criminal trial in which Netanyahu is fighting charges of bribery, fraud, and breach of trust.

Complicating matters further is that Israel lacks a written constitution under and through which the Jewish state's contending sectors could resolve their bitter disagreements. The nation's quasi-constitutional Basic Laws are part of the problem because they were passed by simple majorities, and their status itself is at issue in the battle over the judiciary.

But Israel does have a founding document, and a highly pertinent one at that. At 4:00 p.m. on Friday, May 14, 1948, shortly before the arrival of Shabbat and eight hours before the midnight termination of the British Mandate, David Ben-Gurion read aloud to a group of some 250 dignitaries gathered in the Tel Aviv Museum the Declaration of the Establishment of the State of Israel.

The declaration was drafted amid military hostilities. Also subject to British rule, Palestinian Arabs shared the land with the Jewish inhabitants, but in contrast to the Jews, they rejected the 1947 UN partition plan. Even as the Jews rejoiced in the streets in the late afternoon of May 14 at the birth of the first Jewish state in nearly 2,000 years in the Jewish people's ancestral homeland, the Palestinian Arabs continued their attacks, and the surrounding Arab states prepared their armies to destroy the new country. With Jerusalem besieged and the very survival of Jewish life in the land of Israel at risk, it was all the more remarkable that Israel's founders provided in their declaration the clearest and most authoritative statement of the principles to which the nation-state of the Jewish people would be dedicated.

In *Israel's Declaration of Independence: The History and Political Theory of the Nation's Founding Moment*, Neil Rogachevsky and Dov Zigler perform a great service by clarifying the political significance of Israel's founding principles. The authors—Rogachevsky is a professor at the Straus Center of Yeshiva University, and Zigler is chief international economist at Element Capital—examine the several major drafts of the declaration. They place the declaration in the immediate context of the debates in the pre-Israel Palestine Jewish community over whether to declare a sovereign state, how much weight to give to the borders set forth in the UN partition plan, and the proper recognition of the Jewish people's national and religious character. They review the declaration's legal legacy. Most significantly for the turmoil currently gripping the country, Rogachevsky and Zigler consider the declaration in relation to the modern tradition of freedom, particularly natural rights—the rights all persons share in virtue of their common humanity.

The authors emphasize a crucial change made by Ben-Gurion, who, at the last minute, took charge of editing the final draft. The penultimate draft asserted that the state of Israel would "grant" (*ta'anik*) rights. However, Ben-Gurion—who was nourished on socialism and who gave no evidence of having delved into the writings of Locke, Jefferson, and

Madison—rejected the notion that rights had their roots in the decisions of states: What a state had authority to grant, it also had authority to rescind.

Accordingly, in the key paragraph setting forth the relationship between rights and the Jewish state, the declaration uses the language of "based on" (*mushtata al*), "ensure" (*t'kaim*), "guarantee" (*tavtiach*): "THE STATE OF ISRAEL will be open for Jewish immigration and for the Ingathering of the Exiles; it will foster the development of the country for the benefit of all its inhabitants; it will be based on freedom, justice and peace as envisaged by the prophets of Israel; it will ensure complete equality of social and political rights to all its inhabitants irrespective of religion, race or sex; it will guarantee freedom of religion, conscience, language, education and culture; it will safeguard the Holy Places of all religions; and it will be faithful to the principles of the Charter of the United Nations." Consistent with the US Declaration of Independence, Israel's Declaration of Independence is grounded in the conviction that basic rights inhere in individuals and that governments are duty bound to secure them.

The document does not explicitly mention "democracy." But it commits Israel to democratic institutions by insisting on the establishment of representative government and by stressing that Arab inhabitants would enjoy "full and equal citizenship."

The Israeli Declaration of Independence no more provides a constitution for Israel than does the US Declaration of Independence furnish a constitution for America. Both documents, however, announced a universal standard. In 1859, as civil war loomed, Abraham Lincoln wrote in a letter, "All honor to Jefferson—to the man who, in the concrete pressure of a struggle for national independence by a single people, had the coolness, forecast, and capacity to introduce into a merely revolutionary document, an abstract truth, applicable to all men and all times, and so to embalm it there, that to-day, and in all coming days, it shall be a rebuke and a stumbling-block to the very harbingers of re-appearing tyranny and oppression." Something similar could be said about Ben-Gurion's rejection of the idea, as Israel faced a war of annihilation, that the Jewish state would *grant* rights in favor of the affirmation that Israel would be *based on*, *ensure*, and *guarantee* basic rights. With this affirmation, Israel cast its lot with the free world that regards such rights as inseparable from our humanity.

Reconsideration of the precious inheritance enshrined in Israel's Declaration of Independence could assist both sides in assuaging the rage roiling the country. Bold and conciliatory, the nation's founding document promises not merely a Jewish state, or a free state, or a democratic state, but that Israel will combine and reconcile its diverse elements to form a Jewish and free and democratic state.

21

RESTORING ISRAEL'S FOUNDING BALANCE

April 23, 2023, discussing Saving Israel *by Ari Shavit*

In early January, just days after the swearing in of Prime Minister Benjamin Netanyahu's government but without preparing the nation, Justice Minister Yariv Levin announced an ambitious judicial-reform package aimed at severely restricting the Israeli Supreme Court's power to check the legislative and executive branches. The proposed judicial overhaul sparked massive protests throughout the country. Energized by the center and left including large swaths of the national security community and the high-tech sector, while drawing noteworthy support from the right, the protests are entering their seventeenth week. In late March, amid declining poll numbers, Netanyahu suspended the parliamentary rush to curb the judiciary—the opposition calls it "regime change"—until the Knesset's summer session, which begins May 1. The pause bought Israel time but did not end the unprecedented national crisis.

Netanyahu's April 10 televised speech exhibited conflicting tendencies. On the one hand, he called for national unity. He reported that his government responded forcefully to terrorist attacks in Israel and the territories and to rocket fusillades from Lebanon and Syria and, with the military's full support, would persist. He also promised that judicial reform would maintain protection of individual rights while establishing a sound separation of powers. On the other hand, Netanyahu fanned the flames of disunity. He denounced the previous government for weakening the country and for inviting the new round of hostilities. He also portrayed judicial-reform opponents—encompassing more than half the country, according to recent polls—as undermining Israel's national security and political stability.

Eminent opposition members have also sown discord. To take an egregious example, former Prime Minister Ehud Barak likened Israel's President Isaac Herzog's efforts at mediation to the West's initial appeasement of Nazi Germany. In addition, more than a few flag-waving protesters have raised the stakes: They seek not merely to block the government's judicial reforms but to oust Netanyahu. For several years the center and left have rallied around the slogan "Just not Bibi." Instead of championing alternative policy, they have concentrated on demonizing Netanyahu and, by extension, his supporters.

Citizens' internalization of their political leaders' exhortations to despise the other side may pose the greatest long-term threat to the Jewish state. So argues distinguished Israeli journalist Ari Shavit in a slender volume prompted by the political crisis of which the judicial overhaul, he contends, is only the proximate cause. Composed, he explains, with love, apprehension, and haste, *Saving Israel* (an English translation is in the works) provides a searing analysis of the clash of enmities and empowerment of zealotry in the Jewish state. It also offers an inspiring account of the submerged convictions that still unite a Zionist majority of right and left. And it specifies concrete steps to avert disaster.

A political pamphlet in the old-fashioned sense—capturing unfolding events, distilling essential ideas, touching the heart, elevating debate, and summoning to action—*Saving Israel* stresses that the stakes could scarcely be higher: "The deep crisis of 2023 endangers the Israeli miracle. It threatens to erase our sensational achievements and leave us homeless."

In the shadow of the Holocaust and situated in a cruel neighborhood, recounts Shavit, Israel's courageous and farsighted founders established a state that wove together the Jewish people's magnificent heritage with the modern principles of freedom and democracy. Authoritatively expressed in Israel's 1948 Declaration of Independence, that founding balance remains crucial to the Jewish state's survival. "Israel must be powerful and moral, nationalist and liberal, Jewish and democratic," Shavit writes. "Only the combination of toughness and openness will ensure that neither weakness nor zealotry will bring us to the edge of the abyss."

Facing "impossible conditions," writes Shavit, Israel made itself "a powerful nation against all odds." Under British imperial rule in the decades before Israel's birth, Jews built the physical and institutional infrastructure of a state. They defeated five Arab armies that launched a war of annihilation against their fledgling country. In the following years, Israel accomplished what no nation before or since has even attempted: The country absorbed some 850,000 Mizrachi or Sephardi Jews who had been expelled or were fleeing from their homes in North Africa and the Middle East, which doubled Israel's population. While assimilating this enormous influx of immigrants, Israel constructed world-class hospitals and universities, built the region's most formidable military and high-tech economy, and remained the Middle East's only rights-protecting democracy.

Shavit acknowledges Israel's mistakes. The Jewish state must work harder to integrate the ultra-Orthodox and Arab citizens into the nation's life. It must more fully address many Sephardi Jews' lingering resentments for their community's treatment as second-class citizens at the hands of the mostly Ashkenazi Jews, of European origin, who founded Israel and dominate the country's political institutions, economy, media, and educational system. And it must improve arrangements to provide for both West Bank Palestinians' self-rule and Israeli security.

The right-wing governments that led Israel for most of the last 45 years, Shavit argues, preserved and obscured the nation's founding balance. Elected prime minister in 1977, conservative Zionist Menachem Begin kept faith with the imperative to harmonize Israel's Jewish, free, and democratic character. So, too, until recently, did his right-wing Zionist successors—Yitzhak Shamir, Ariel Sharon, and Benjamin Netanyahu. At the same time, exploitation of resentments for political gain by both right and left has divided Israel into bitter and belligerent tribes: Ashkenazi and Mizrachi, religious and secular, Jew and Arab, pro-Netanyahu and anti-Netanyahu.

Conciliation has become a dirty word. Many on the right have not forgiven the left for the mid-1990s Oslo Accords, culminating in the early 2000s in the devastating Second Intifada, and for the 2005 Gaza evacuation. Meanwhile, many in the center and on the left revile the right for aggressive settlement policies in Judea and Samaria, which push Israel toward a single state between the Jordan River and the Mediterranean Sea that would lose either its Jewish character or its free and democratic character, or both.

In November 2022, according to Shavit, Netanyahu—a defendant in a long-running criminal trial for bribery, fraud, and breach of trust—formed a coalition that shattered the nation's founding balance. For the first time in Israel's history, half the coalition comprised ultra-Orthodox and religious ultranationalist parties. Consequently, Israel's most extreme elements could, for the first time, hold the prime minister hostage on essential matters.

Notwithstanding the coalition's solemn talk of restoring democracy, its judicial overhaul would shift power from one minority to another, Shavit observes. Yes, the Supreme Court overreached in the 1990s and in the decades since by adopting a highly expansive understanding of judicial review. Yes, the judicial selection committee's composition long allowed high court justices to replenish their ranks with like-minded left-leaning justices, though reforms instituted in 2008 gave the governing coalition and the legal establishment a veto over appointments. And yes, the high court has used its sweeping jurisdiction to impose progressive outcomes contrary to majority will.

However, as *Yedioth Ahronoth* columnist Ben-Dror Yemini and Yeshiva University Professor Neil Rogachevsky have also pointed out, the nation's coalition government system, coupled with Israeli society's distinctive fractures, also enables other minorities to dictate law and public policy.

Judicial overhaul opponents rightly fear that a diminished court will enable the ultra-Orthodox, who constitute approximately 13.5 percent of Israel's population, to entrench their schools' substantial state subsidies, persist in omitting core subjects from their schools' curricula, and make permanent their exemption from military service.[1] Judicial overhaul opponents also understandably suspect that the religious ultranationalist minority will take advantage of an enfeebled court to accelerate construction beyond the major blocs in Judea and Samaria.

Shavit sees a way out. Israel's Zionist majority—encompassing significant swaths of the right and left, Ashkenazim and Sephardim, traditionalists and nationalists, and ultra-Orthodox and religious nationalists—must band together. Committed to rights and democracy, the Zionist majority's several components must cease internal feuding, put national interest ahead of personal ambition and party politics, and form a broad-based coalition. This new "Zionist covenant" calls for a reconfiguration of "the Israeli political map" in which the decisive opposition would "no longer be right against left but moderates against extremists."

Painful concessions will be necessary, Shavit stresses. Netanyahu, who has licensed zealotry and has leveraged grudges and grievances, must

1 Judah Ari Gross, "Haredim Are Fastest-Growing Population, Will Be 16% of Israelis by Decade's End," *Times of Israel,* January 2, 2023, https://www.timesofisrael.com/haredim-are-fastest-growing-population-will-be-16-of-israelis-by-decades-end.

prepare his fellow conservative Zionists for a coalition that does not depend on the ultra-Orthodox and the religious ultranationalist minorities. Meanwhile, the center and center-left must set aside their loathing of the prime minister and retract their refusal to enter into a power-sharing agreement with him. Current polls suggest that a center-right-led coalition, embracing the sober left and joined by the ultra-Orthodox and by rights-respecting religious nationalists, could form a broad and stable government.

The national unity government envisaged by Shavit would enjoy the democratic legitimacy to pursue the new majority position in Israel: Judicial reform is necessary but must establish a stable and effective separation of powers that preserves an independent, rights-protecting judiciary. This institutional reform would do more than avert the present crisis. It would invigorate the nation's founding balance, which would empower conservative and progressive Zionists to cooperate in fortifying a Jewish, free, and democratic Israel.

22

THE ULTRA-ORTHODOX CHALLENGE IN ISRAEL

May 28, 2023, discussing "Without Evidence: The Problem Is Not the Ultra-Orthodox but Rather the 'It Will Be OK' Camp" by Shmuel Rosner

It is easy to understand why the controversy over the 2023–2024 budget passed in the early hours last Wednesday by Prime Minister Benjamin Netanyahu's government has not received the attention it deserves. Five months of unprecedented protests sparked by the judicial reforms proposed by the governing coalition in early January, combined with the Israel Defense Forces' deftly executed five-day early-May Gaza operation, known as Shield and Arrow, preoccupied the nation and foreign observers. Yet the budget's extraordinary outlays for Israel's ultra-Orthodox community intensify the fears not only of Tel Aviv's largely secular elites but also of Israelis of diverse political affiliations and religious orientations who believe that the coalition's policies endanger freedom, democracy, and prosperity in the Jewish state.

According to an analysis in the *Jerusalem Post,* the budget contains good and bad, as well as the ugly.[1] On the positive side of the ledger, the

1 Eliav Breuer, "The Good, the Bad and the Ugly of Israel's 2023–2024 Budget," *Jerusalem Post*, May 19, 2023, https://www.jpost.com/israel-news/politics-and-diplomacy/article-743514.

budget includes a massive infrastructure bill that reduces bureaucracy and regulation, and features measures to increase municipalities' incentives to build residential housing, a plan to remove costly regulations on food and toiletries, steps to streamline health insurance and lower its cost, and reform of small-business taxation. On the negative side, the budget high-handedly transfers municipal taxes from more prosperous cities to less prosperous ones (which tend to vote for coalition members) while excluding Arab cities; waters down, in apparent response to lobbyists' exertions, measures originally proposed to reduce the price of food and toiletries; and is forecast to increase the deficit.

The ugly aspect stems from the substantial transfer of wealth to the ultra-Orthodox, a transfer that increases incentives for the community to cut itself off from the larger Israeli society and to persist in its poverty. After the approximately $270 billion budget passed last week, the *Times of Israel* reported that "NIS 3.7 billion [approximately $995 million] will go to increasing the budget for stipends for full-time Haredi [ultra-Orthodox] yeshiva students who receive exemptions from military service." In addition, "NIS 1.2 billion [approximately $323 million] is budgeted for private, non-supervised Haredi educational institutions, many of which do not teach core subjects such as math and English, while additional funds will go to the official Haredi education system, and for construction of buildings for religious purposes and supporting Haredi culture and identity."[2] In other words the new budget empowers a community—in which families average 6.6 children, most young people neither serve in the army nor complete alternative national service, and half the adult men devote themselves to the study of sacred Jewish texts rather than to gainful employment—to evade the basic education that would enable them to participate in, and shoulder their fair share of responsibility for, maintaining and defending Israel.

---

2 Carrie Keller-Lynn, "Knesset Approves 2023–2024 Budget in All-Night Vote, Patching Coalition Rift," *Times of Israel,* May 24, 2023, https://www.timesofisrael.com/knesset-approves-2023-2024-budget-in-all-night-vote-patching-coalition-rift.

In his column one weekend ago in the Hebrew-language daily *Maariv*, my friend Shmuel Rosner clarified with characteristic fair-mindedness the dangers embedded in the state subsidies and exemptions long provided to the ultra-Orthodox and further entrenched by the new budget. "Israel's Central Bureau of Statistics," according to Rosner, "determined that the proportion of ultra-Orthodox in Israel will reach a third of the population by the middle of the 2060s." But the demographic situation is worse, he maintains. That's because the statistics overlook the likelihood that the rapid growth of the ultra-Orthodox, which would bring about greater political power that would further expand and entrench their subsidies and exemptions, would prompt a non-ultra-Orthodox flight from Israel. "The Israelis who stare at the process that is unfolding in front of their eyes," writes Rosner, "are pale, impotent, angry, dispirited, and gripped by the widespread feeling of erosion and retreat throughout the liberal West."

Rosner identifies four informal schools of thought in Israel concerning the ultra-Orthodox challenge. The first school sees no problem because it favors a more ultra-Orthodox and generally more religious Israel. The second, typical of the non-ultra-Orthodox right, maintains that "it will be okay" because slowly but surely the ultra-Orthodox will change and increasingly participate in the economy and in defending the country. The third, common from the center-right to the center-left, declares that Israel must take swift action to reduce the damage to its free and democratic character. The fourth, a counsel of despair increasingly heard on the hard left, insists that freedom and democracy in Israel have been routed and cannot be restored.

Rosner argues that the future of liberal democracy in the Jewish state depends on the second and third schools: the non-ultra-Orthodox right, who believe that time will moderate the ultra-Orthodox and gradually bring about their incorporation into the Israeli mainstream, and the center-right to center-left, who advocate decisive action to avert disaster. The first and fourth schools—those who look forward to a future dominated by the ultra-Orthodox and those who believe that all is lost—lack motivation to undertake the arduous work of democratic politics: coalition building, policy analysis, legal reform, and constitutional design.

Nevertheless, emphasizes Rosner, the "it will be okay" optimism of the non-ultra-Orthodox right poses a major obstacle to a potential alliance with those spanning the center-right to center-left and their catastrophe-is-imminent sense of urgency. Because of their sympathy for the ultra-Orthodox communities and their perception that the ultra-Orthodox are enduring political partners, the non-ultra-Orthodox right has a strong interest in avoiding a showdown with the ultra-Orthodox. Moreover, the non-ultra-Orthodox right thinks that a showdown is unnecessary. They contend that, thanks to the cell phones in which the ultra-Orthodox indulge, the digital world will leave its mark on the community, fostering greater openness to Israeli society and the wider world. And the non-ultra-Orthodox right believes that difficult-to-discern but "deep currents of change" flowing through the ultra-Orthodox community will amplify these salutary developments.

Rosner remains unconvinced. After all, claims have been put forward for at least 20 years about the transformative effects of "deep currents of change" with little detectable impact on ultra-Orthodox political demands.

Unlike many critics, Rosner insists that the ultra-Orthodox are not the problem. They pursue their interests as they understand them through the democratic process, he soberly observes. Nor does Rosner fault the dispirited hard left who are immobilized by their despair. And he welcomes those stretching from the center-right to the center-left who have taken to the streets in the tens of thousands weekend after weekend since January to demonstrate in opposition to the government's proposed judicial overhaul. The problem, he maintains, is the non-ultra-Orthodox right. They provide the crucial votes for the state subsidies and exemptions that enable the ultra-Orthodox to shirk the normal responsibilities of citizenship in a free and democratic nation.

At the same time, Rosner especially likes and admires the non-ultra-Orthodox right. "This is the camp of good men and women, the nicest, most patriotic, and most sympathetic camp," he writes. "But in this matter, they are a camp of messianic fools." Rosner's assessment is unsparing: "'It will be okay' is not policy, 'it will be okay' is messianism. Especially when it is impossible to find a hint of evidence that it will be okay." Indeed, according to Rosner, the evidence points in the opposite direction: "After all, the ultra-Orthodox, having obtained a little power and sitting comfortably in the coalition, could apply pressure on the government to receive what they want. Did they restrain their demands? Did they compromise on their requirements? Did they reveal sensitivity to their rivals' worries?" The answers are no.

Such self-serving conduct, reminds Rosner, does not distinguish the ultra-Orthodox. In eschewing restraint, declining to compromise, and disregarding their rivals' sensitivities, the ultra-Orthodox use their increasing influence to fortify their preferred way of life—as interest groups are wont to do in democratic politics. It is the non-ultra-Orthodox right, Rosner contends, who must revise their stance. Addressing them in particular, he argues that as the ultra-Orthodox continue to grow in numbers and power, "they apparently will not change in the direction you thought but rather in the opposite direction. They will change, and change Israel in accordance with their vision."

That vision is not sustainable over the long run. Israel's vibrant high-tech sector and its powerful and valiant military enable the country to flourish in a hostile and unforgiving neighborhood. But Israel's innovators and producers, along with its warriors—in many cases they are one and the same—will be increasingly reluctant to lend their ingenuity and resources to the economy of, and put their limbs and lives on the line for, a country that retreats from the basic requirements of freedom and democracy.

Accordingly, it is also in the long-term interest of the non-ultra-Orthodox right, others who wish to see the ultra-Orthodox way of life flourish in Israel, and Israel's ultra-Orthodox themselves to support laws and policies that secure individual rights, shared responsibilities, and democratic self-government in the Jewish state.

23

RESTORING CONDITIONS IN ISRAEL THAT MAKE COMPROMISE VIABLE

September 3, 2023, discussing "Israel's Elites Revolt Against Democracy" by Gadi Taub

TEL AVIV—The security, stability, and prosperity of a pluralistic, rights-protecting democracy depend on citizens' disposition to compromise. A nation's success in securing outcomes that may satisfy no camp entirely but with which all can live represents a substantial political achievement. Salutary compromise stems in significant measure from the people's commitment to widely held norms and principles and their shared sense of participating in a common enterprise that transcends the interests of this group or that tribe.

These tried-and-true maxims apply to the rights-protecting and democratic nation-state of the Jewish people. Yet since early January, when Israeli Prime Minister Benjamin Netanyahu's coalition government proposed sweeping judicial reforms, prompting tens of thousands to take to the streets every Saturday night for almost eight months and counting, prominent voices on both sides have disparaged compromise as ignominious defeat. The retreat to the extremes presents a serious internal threat to Israel's security, stability, and prosperity.

Many supporters of Netanyahu's governing coalition reject further compromise in reining in what many—and not only conservatives—regard as Israel's hyperactivist Supreme Court. In the judgment of Netanyahu's allies, the compromises that have already been forced upon their camp amount to surrender to arrogant elites unwilling to accept their inability to win elections and mark a betrayal of the democratic principle of majority rule. Plenty of Netanyahu's supporters are determined to remember the indignity and, when political circumstances allow, to exact revenge.

Meanwhile, many opponents of the governing coalition's judicial overhaul remain adamant that further compromise in preventing what they call regime change is out of the question. That's because, they believe, the Netanyahu government seeks to extinguish the high court's independence.

Neutering the court, opponents contend, would empower extremist members of the governing coalition. It would prevent the court from blocking application of Israeli sovereignty to the whole of Judea and Samaria, which would incorporate 2.5 to 3 million West Bank Palestinians into the Jewish state. It would thwart judicial review of the entrenchment of exemptions from the normal obligations of Israeli citizenship, including military service and gainful employment, for the rapidly growing ultra-Orthodox community. And it would enable a Netanyahu-led Knesset to insulate the prime minister from or even short-circuit the criminal indictments he is currently fighting in court.

Mutual contempt is consuming the nation's common ground. Many on both sides advance compelling arguments for their positions while denying legitimacy to the other's concerns. Many on both sides express anger and resentment over how their communities have been disrespected while turning a deaf ear to the other's wounds and grievances. Many on both sides have resolved to mount a last stand in defense of the nation they love while denouncing opponents as intransigent foes who pose an existential menace to the country.

In "Israel's Elites Revolt Against Democracy," my friend Gadi Taub—a best-selling author in Israel, as well as a historian, journalist, and podcast and radio talk show host—forcefully states the governing coalition's case.[1] "The protest movement that arose to defend the court's power (and its backers among the country's economic and military elite) are together attempting to block the redemocratization of Israeli politics, as the reforms intended to do," he maintains. The protesters' real goal, according to Taub, is to oust Netanyahu. Reservists declining to report to duty and warnings by retired commanders, including former chiefs of staff and heads of the Mossad and Shabak (Israel's internal security service), about declining morale constitute an unfolding "military coup," in Taub's judgment. Controversy over the recently passed curtailment of the court's ability to invalidate ministerial actions and appointments as unreasonable "is not about saving Israel from a future theocratic right-wing dictatorship," he writes. "It is about releasing Israel's democracy from the already existing juristocratic rule."

Taub anticipates a protracted struggle. "The road to freeing Israeli democracy from the tyranny of the country's Supreme Court and its auxiliaries is going to be long and difficult," he asserts. "This is not only because the court is not going to give up any of its powers voluntarily. It is also because Israel's progressive elite rules through the court, and it is now thrashing wildly, threatening to burn the house down, tear the army apart, weaponize the law, and bring economic ruin in the country, if the plebs dare to challenge the patricians' juristocracy."

Taub's condemnation of Israel's high court and censure of the opposition reflect important issues of judicial overreach and opposition zeal. Yet only some, probably a small minority but including well-known figures, among the protesters fit his withering description of progressive authoritarians. The bigger problem is that treating Israel as a pure democracy despite its founding as a rights-protecting democracy skews Taub's analysis.

---

1 Gadi Taub, "Israel's Elites Revolt against Democracy," *Tablet magazine*, August 16, 2023, https://www.tabletmag.com/sections/israel-middle-east/articles/israel-elite-revolt-against-democracy.

First, Taub gives the impression that Netanyahu's governing coalition secured an unambiguous mandate to undertake far-reaching judicial reform. However, the democratic legitimacy of the coalition's ambitions to substantially alter the relation between government branches is dubious. Notwithstanding opposition leaders' fears, Netanyahu scarcely mentioned judicial reform during last autumn's campaign. Nor did he make an issue of the judiciary in the previous four elections Israel has held since the beginning of 2019 or, for that matter, as prime minister from 2009 to 2019. Netanyahu's coalition, moreover, lacks a mandate for sweeping change of any sort. Last November, his bloc won the opportunity to form a coalition, thanks to a mere 30,000-vote margin, garnering 49.57 percent of the total votes. (Some 300,000 ballots cast for the left-wing party Meretz and the Arab party Balad were wasted because they received too few to qualify for representation in the Knesset.) And for several months, the polls have indicated that a majority opposes the coalition's reforms and supports the opposition.

Second, Taub neglects the paucity of the Israeli political system's checks and balances. Israel not only lacks a written constitution; it is also bereft of a meaningful separation between the legislative branch and the executive branch because in practice the prime minister heads both. In *The Federalist* No. 47, James Madison, following "the celebrated Montesquieu," argues that when any two of the three principal powers of government are placed in a single department, "the fundamental principles of a free constitution are subverted." While thoughtful members of the opposition agree with the right that reform of Israel's highly assertive judiciary is imperative, Israel particularly needs a strong and independent high court to check abuse of power because its executive and legislative branches largely function as a unit.

Third, Taub overlooks the teaching, as old as Aristotle and adapted for modern rights-protecting democracies by *The Federalist*, that the worthy democratic principle of majority rule must be tempered by combining it with other worthy political claims. One such is the protection of individual rights, which limits majority will. A specific implication in the Israeli context of the imperative to harmonize the competing interests and principles is that the concerns of the country's tech sector and entrepreneurial class, which have become vital to Israeli prosperity, and of its people's army, which is indispensable to Israel's security, must be taken into account rather than derided in devising major reform of basic governmental institutions.

Fourth, while facing a generally progressive permanent bureaucracy, media establishment, and system of higher education, the right in Israel cannot persuasively portray itself as a victim incapable of translating election victories into political achievements because of an imperial court and its bureaucratic, media, and academic enablers. One need look no further than Netanyahu's authoritative assessment. Last year, in *Bibi: My Story*, Israel's longest-serving prime minister celebrated, and rightly so, his fostering of a prosperous economy, which sustains a powerful military that has buttressed the nation's diplomacy. Furthermore, Netanyahu's current coalition partners have effectively pursued their long-term political aims with his Likud Party's assistance. Religious ultranationalist members of Finance Minister Bezalel Smotrich's Religious Zionist Party and of National Security Minister Itamar Ben-Gvir's Jewish Power party have seen Jewish settlement in Judea and Samaria steadily expand. Meanwhile, the ultra-Orthodox have won increased state subsidies for their community's separatist way of life while maintaining control over the Chief Rabbinate, which exercises jurisdiction over Jewish marriage, divorce, burial, and conversion; Jewish immigration; and more.

In "Israel Is in Danger from a Radicalized Center," Yedidia Stern acknowledges his side's extremist tendencies.[2] An opponent of the coalition's judicial reforms—and Jewish People Policy Institute president and Bar-Ilan University law professor—Stern warns that notwithstanding his

2 Yedidia Stern, "Israel Is in Danger from a Radicalized Center," *Jerusalem Post, August 18, 2023, https://www.jpost.com/opinion/article-755197.*

sympathy for their anguish, volunteer reservists refusing to report for duty, doctors planning to emigrate, and those calling for the cantonization of Israel destabilize the nation and undercut the Zionist commitment to provide a home for all Jews in a free and democratic Israel. One could add to Stern's list of dangers those who encourage intimidation of lawmakers and ministers through threats of, or actual, violence.

The coalition and opposition are on track for a head-on collision on September 12 when all 15 Supreme Court judges hear appeals of the new restrictions on the court's use of the reasonableness doctrine. To avoid a genuine constitutional crisis, the court must find ways to both uphold the rule of law and author restraints on the judiciary's own excesses. And Netanyahu must honor his postelection promise to "set up a national government that will look after all the citizens of Israel, without exception, because the state is all of ours"[3] by concentrating his formidable intelligence and political talents on restoring conditions in Israel that make compromise viable.

3 "Netanyahu Promises 'a National Government,' Says He'll Act to Heal Internal Rifts," *Times of Israel*, November 2, 2022, https://www.timesofisrael.com/liveblog_entry/netanyahu-promises-a-nationalist-government-says-hell-act-to-heal-internal-rifts.

24

STEADYING ISRAEL BY RECALIBRATING THE SEPARATION OF POWERS

September 10, 2023, discussing "The Moment Before the Constitutional Chaos" by Raz Nizri

On September 12 all 15 judges of Israel's Supreme Court—never before has the full complement of high-court judges sat as one body—are scheduled to hear challenges to the contentious legislation enacted in July by Prime Minister Benjamin Netanyahu's governing coalition. The only part of the judicial overhaul proposed by Justice Minister Yariv Levin in early January that has been passed by the Knesset amends Israel's Basic Law: The Judiciary. The amendment bars the court from invalidating ministerial and cabinet decisions on the grounds of the judicial standard of reasonableness. Netanyahu has declined to say whether he would obey what would be an extraordinary step by the high court—overturning the amendment—though on September 7 he shared on social media Knesset Speaker Amir Ohana's speech from the day before declaring that the Knesset "won't submissively allow itself to be trampled." With large-scale protests throughout the country entering their ninth month, military reservists refusing to serve, the threat mounting of draft-age Israelis declining to report for military service, and private investment in Israel—internal and from abroad—declining, the coming Supreme Court showdown may well drive Israel further into uncharted territory.

In August in the Hebrew daily newspaper *Yedioth Ahronoth*, attorney Raz Nizri provided a particularly sober account of the crisis's origins and character and offered judicious counsel on how to escape it. In "The Moment Before the Constitutional Chaos: The Approaching Nightmare Scenario and the Way to Prevent It," the former deputy attorney general observed that a high-court decision is unlikely until after the four weeks of celebration of Jewish holidays from mid-September to mid-October. However, Nizri warned, if in midautumn the Supreme Court issues a ruling invalidating the Knesset's restrictions on the court's use of the reasonableness doctrine—as, last week, Attorney General Gali Baharav Miara urged it to do in a formal legal opinion—the controversy that has engulfed the nation could spin out of control.

Nizri's nightmare scenario is all too realistic. The governing coalition would likely respond to a decision striking down or trimming the new law by enacting legislation that explicitly prohibits the court from reviewing Basic Laws. In response to the inevitable legal challenges, the Supreme Court could declare null and void the legislature's duly enacted prohibition on the court's considering the legality of Basic Laws. Who decides then who has the final word on Basic Laws' legal status? Alternatively, the court might defy the new law by rejecting a decision by the governing coalition—say, to oust the head of the Bank of Israel—on the grounds of unreasonableness. Who then would be responsible for determining who sets the interest rates on government loans?

In either case, says Nizri, furious Israelis will fill the streets. Some will pledge allegiance to the high court, others to the Knesset majority. The standoff will have no obvious resolution. "The source of the authority in the country will have become unclear," writes Nizri, "even as it will become doubtful whether a country remains in which we will be able to clarify and answer the question."

Such nightmare scenarios are avoidable, argues Nizri, but only if both the governing coalition and the high court face up to their roles in bringing the nation to the brink. To undertake a "conciliatory tango," the governing coalition must recognize that its judicial overhaul puts individual rights at risk in Israel by empowering the majority to govern as it pleases almost without limits. At the same time, the high court must acknowledge that it has weakened democracy in Israel by acting for decades as if it is authorized, almost without limits, to intervene in Israeli politics based on moral and political judgments masquerading as legal reasoning.

In Nizri's view the coalition bears greater responsibility for the current crisis because it controls executive and legislative authority. While the pendulum had swung too far in the court's direction, he argues, Netanyahu's government proceeded recklessly, both in the extremity of its proposals and in its hasty and heavy-handed efforts to enact them. Impervious to separation-of-powers imperatives as well as to the need to maintain political cohesiveness in a divided nation, the coalition would swing the pendulum too far in the opposite direction with its judicial overhaul. It would undercut, in the name of majority rule, the court's ability to serve as a serious check on the excesses to which all legislative and executive branches are prone, particularly when, as in Israel, they function in practice as a single branch of government.

The governing coalition's errors, however, do not absolve the Supreme Court from its share of responsibility for unleashing the forces that have been tearing the country apart. Nor does the indispensability to Israel of a strong and independent judiciary, not least because recognition that Israel's military acts subject to the high court's review shields the nation's soldiers and diplomats from investigation and prosecution by international institutions, erase the court's culpability. Decades of judicial activism have seen the court expand the range of issues that it regards as justiciable and eliminate barriers to standing, allowing merely interested parties to bring challenges before it rather than only those directly harmed in a case or controversy. The court's sustained overreach, coupled with its arrogant dismissal of criticism, argues Nizri, has impaired the rule of law in Israel by damaging the judicial branch's public legitimacy.

It is against this explosive combination of causes—the governing coalition's recklessness and imperviousness and the high court's overreach and arrogance—that this week all 15 Supreme Court judges will consider the fraught question of whether they have authority to review the Knesset's recent amendment to the Basic Law: The Judiciary.

At first glance it seems that the court does not. It is settled law in Israel, according to Nizri, that the Supreme Court may invalidate regular legislation that conflicts with Basic Laws but lacks the authority to review Basic Laws.

The puzzle is that Israel's Basic Laws both are and are not special. On the one hand, Basic Laws enjoy quasi-constitutional status because the Knesset enacts them pursuant to its "constitutive authority" to pass laws one at a time that will eventually form a written constitution. On the other hand, Israel's Basic Laws become law based not on a supermajority but, like regular laws, with the support of a simple majority. In contrast, in the United States, constitutional amendments require proposals from two-thirds of both houses of Congress or from conventions in two-thirds of the states and ratification by three-quarters of the states.

In recent years, however, some Israeli high-court judges, following the lead of American law professors and courts around the world, have fashioned arguments, reports Nizri, according to which, in exceptional circumstances, the court may invalidate a Basic Law on the grounds that it represents an "unconstitutional constitutional amendment"—that is, one that conflicts with "fundamental values of the system" or involves a "misuse of the Knesset's authority as a constitutive authority." Such arguments in the Israeli context, maintains Nizri, are at best underdeveloped.

Were the high court to invoke such a novel constitutional theory to overturn the Knesset's circumscription of judges' authority to apply the reasonableness doctrine, it would divide the judges, according to Nizri, producing a split decision that "would be greeted with a sigh of relief from half the people and with horror from the other half" and would trigger "a constitutional and social earthquake."

To prevent the chaos, concludes Nizri, both the governing coalition and the high court must exercise restraint on behalf of the public interest. The coalition must resist the voices on the street and in the government that demand it barrel ahead with the whole package of judicial reforms. The court must resist other voices on the street and among protest leaders who "hope it will 'save the country' by using the doomsday weapon of nullifying a Basic Law."

Nizri would have the coalition inform the court of its intention to seek, in cooperation with the opposition, wide agreement on judicial reform, including a less sweeping version of the recent revision of the reasonableness doctrine. If the sides agreed to further negotiations, Nizri would advise the court to postpone its September 12 hearing. That would give the coalition and the opposition time to reach a workable compromise.

President Herzog has undertaken a last-ditch effort to bring together the coalition and opposition.[1] At this late date, he faces daunting odds.

Nevertheless, the short-term compromise that Nizri envisaged in August still represents the most promising path forward, not least because it would set the state stage for drafting and passing, at long last, "Basic Law: Legislation." Nizri envisages legislation agreed to by the coalition and opposition that would entrench a definition of Basic Laws, the procedure for enacting them, and whether and under what circumstances the high court can invalidate or modify them.

Such desperately needed legislation would do more than legislate. By joining forces to recalibrate the separation of powers through deliberation

1 Carrie Keller-Lynn, "What Herzog's Overhaul Plan Means, and the Impediments to a Potential Breakthrough," *Times of Israel,* September 5, 2023, https://www.timesofisrael.com/what-herzogs-overhaul-plan-means-and-the-impediments-to-a-potential-breakthrough.

and consensus, the coalition and opposition would provide a model for—and begin the long, hard work of—steadying the nation.

25

THE 10/7 ATTACKS

October 11, 2023

On October 10, in an address to the nation, President Joe Biden pledged unequivocal US support for Israel. Iran-backed Hamas had perpetrated an "atrocity on an appalling scale," said the president. "We stand with Israel," he declared. In closing, he reiterated, "Let there be no doubt, the United States has Israel's back."

Biden promised to "make sure Israel has what it needs to take care of its citizens, defend itself, and respond to this attack." He indicated that he had encouraged Israeli Prime Minister Benjamin Netanyahu to proceed in a manner that was "swift, decisive, and overwhelming." America's commander in chief stressed that his administration was "surging additional military assistance, including ammunition and interceptors to replenish Iron Dome" and was "going to make sure that Israel does not run out of these critical assets to defend its cities and its citizens."

Painfully aware that Americans were among those kidnapped by the terrorists, the president said that he had advised his team to cooperate closely with Israeli counterparts on bringing the hostages home.

Joe Biden rose to the grim occasion. Many difficult days lie ahead for Israel in coming to grips with the origins and horror of the 10/7 attacks, defeating the jihadists, and handling the daunting geopolitical ramifications.

On the Jewish Sabbath—which coincided with the holiday of Shemini Atzeret, and almost exactly 50 years to the day from Egypt's surprise attack in what came to be known as the Yom Kippur War—Hamas, joined by jihadists from Gaza's many other terrorist organizations, launched a surprise attack that inflicted the greatest single-day loss of civilian life in Israel's history. The first-day death toll now exceeds 1,000; it includes some 260 young people gunned down by the terrorists in the early morning light at an all-night music fest in the desert near Gaza and the execution of babies. More than 2,000 were wounded during that awful day. In the first 24 hours, Hamas savages also seized and transported to Gaza at least 100 hostages and perhaps considerably more—children, teenagers, young adults, and senior citizens—while raping women and desecrating corpses.

Hamas's 10/7 attacks on Israel have been compared with al-Qaeda's 9/11 attacks on the United States. In a sense, the devastation in Israel—a nation less than one-thirtieth the size of the United States—is much greater. On 9/11 al-Qaeda jihadists killed approximately 3,000 Americans, wounded thousands more, and took no hostages. If the United States were to absorb an attack that affected the same proportion of the population as the 10/7 attacks affected in Israel, it would mean more than 30,000 people murdered in cold blood, more than 60,000 wounded, and more than 3,000 taken hostage. In a country situated in a vastly more hostile neighborhood than the United States, Hamas's rampage through Israel's southern border towns, moshavim, and kibbutzim in pursuit of civilians to murder, rape, humiliate, and kidnap, along with the terrorists' bombardment of south and central Israel with thousands of rockets, have provoked a swifter and likely more devastating response from Israel than America's initial rout of the Taliban in Afghanistan and eventual removal of Saddam Hussein's regime in Iraq.

Hours after Hamas killers paraglided over and broke through Israel's security barrier—and sailed around it to invade Israel by sea—Netanyahu put Hamas's October 7 attack in a new category. The four previous major rounds of armed conflict with Hamas since 2005, when Israel withdrew every soldier and civilian from Gaza, had been limited operations designed to suppress the jihadists' rocket fire on civilians. This conflict was different. "Citizens of Israel, we are at war, not in an operation or in rounds of conflict, but at war," he stated. "I have ordered an extensive mobilization of reservists and that we return fire of a magnitude that the enemy has not known."

Later in the evening, in formal remarks to the nation, Netanyahu effectively scrapped his long-standing policy, which has been to contain Hamas and even work with Gaza's Islamist rulers to maintain the status quo. Israel's new aim is to drastically alter the status quo. "What happened today has not been seen in Israel," the prime minister stated. Netanyahu used unprecedented language to promise an unprecedented response to the unprecedented invasion and massacre of civilians: "The Israel Defense Forces will act immediately to destroy Hamas's capabilities," Netanyahu said in a televised address. "We will cripple them mercilessly and avenge this black day they have brought upon Israel and its citizens."

In brief remarks Defense Minister Yoav Gallant echoed the prime minister's harsh assessment and stern resolve. In its monstrous attack on Israel's civilian population, Gallant said, Hamas committed a "grave error" for which "it will pay the price." Unlike "in the past," Israel "will act with full strength" to "change the face of reality in the Gaza Strip 50 years forward."

Oscillating between heartbreak and rage, Israelis across the political spectrum support the government's war aims.

Following the intelligence failures that permitted thousands of Hamas killers to break into Israel, the slowness of Israel's initial military response, the heroism of Israeli civilians, and the courageous and painstaking efforts by security forces to rescue the communities under siege in southern Israel and track down the remaining terrorists, Israel is gearing up for a major military campaign. Since the morning of October 7, waves of Israeli airstrikes have hit hundreds of Hamas targets in Gaza. The government mobilized 300,000 reservists in 48 hours; another 60,000 were called up by the war's fourth day. Tanks and other weapons have flowed into the south. Meanwhile, by midweek, US supplies of munitions and military equipment had reached Israel, an American carrier strike group had arrived in the eastern Mediterranean, and the United States had increased the number of its fighter aircraft in the region.

The military offensive that Netanyahu and Gallant promised is bound to be extended and costly. As Israel prosecutes its just war of self-defense against Hamas barbarism, three considerations should be kept in mind.

First, the real cause of the October 7 attacks is the jihad that Hamas was founded to undertake against Israel. Yes, Israel has been embroiled with internal strife since January, and yes, Iran funds Hamas and apparently helped plan the assault on Israel. Those realities form part of a full account of the 10/7 attacks and of the failures of Israel intelligence and deterrence. But they acquire their meaning within Hamas's Islamist religious war against Israel. As Andrew McCarthy has explained time and again, jihad for Hamas "is not a personal struggle but a collective one, the obligation to wage a holy war to impose the sharia system on the world, and especially to impose it on territory, such as Israel, that Muslims consider to be Islamic."

The 1988 Hamas Covenant states, "The Islamic Resistance Movement is a distinguished Palestinian movement, whose allegiance is to Allah, and whose way of life is Islam. It strives to raise the banner of Allah over every inch of Palestine, for under the wing of Islam followers of all religions can coexist in security and safety where their lives, possessions and rights are concerned." Hamas does not seek to liberate Gaza but to conquer Israel. Notwithstanding the pretty words about religious coexistence in Hamas's charter, everywhere jihadists have raised Allah's banner, they have persecuted and killed Jews, Christians, and other religious minorities.

Second, Hamas has grotesquely violated the international laws of war, and Israel has every right under those laws to disarm Hamas, dismantle its terrorist networks, and destroy its capacity to wage war against the Jewish state. Hebrew University Law School Professor Yuval Shany observed that "Hamas has committed a long list of crimes in this attack" that "have been documented, including the killing of civilians, taking civilians captive, and abusing the bodies of civilians and soldiers."[1] That observation does not go nearly far enough. Hamas also commits war crimes with the thousands of rockets that it showers on Israel's civilian population. And Hamas commits war crimes by positioning its offices, armaments, and operations in civilian areas in Gaza. Consequently, the injuries to and deaths of Gaza Palestinians resulting from Israel's air strikes on Hamas targets, and from the coming ground campaign intended to vanquish Hamas, stem as a legal matter from Hamas's war crimes and are presumptively Hamas's responsibility.

Third, the United States has a vital national security interest for Israel, as President Biden told Prime Minister Netanyahu, to defeat Hamas swiftly, decisively, and overwhelmingly. This would also deal a major blow to Iran's quest to impose its brand of Islamic theocracy on the whole of the Middle East. It would encourage the Saudis to expand cooperation with Israel and the United States. And with the Chinese Communist Party closely monitoring events, it would advance the interests of freedom and democracy in the region and show that in a moment of great danger, friends and partners can count on America.

Biden's pledge of unequivocal US support for Israel is just and necessary because Israel's cause is just and because America's interests are

---

1 Jeremy Sharon, "Footage of Hamas Assault on Civilians Shows Likely War Crimes, Experts Say," *Times of Israel,* October 8, 2023, https://www.timesofisrael.com/footage-of-hamas-assault-on-civilians-shows-likely-war-crimes-experts-say.

advanced by Israel's achieving a crushing victory over the savage Hamas jihadists and their nefarious Iranian paymasters.

26

THE CONTEXT OF HAMAS APOLOGISTS' CALL FOR CONTEXT

November 5, 2023

Strategists close to the front seek to understand the constellation of circumstances and ideas that provoke hostilities. So, too, must responsible commentators far from danger assess the adversaries' rival claims. The need to grasp a war's wider frame goes for Iran-backed Hamas's 10/7 massacres and Israel's exercise of its right of self-defense.

No shortage of Hamas apologists insist that the jihadists' mass atrocities perpetrated against civilians in southern Israel and their indiscriminate rocket attacks extending to much of the center of the country must be placed in context. Indeed, context is crucial. But the apologists don't provide a reliable account of Hamas's motives, ideas, goals, and conduct; a reasonable summary of Israel's response; or a scrupulous overview of the Israeli-Arab conflict, not least Islamist enmity toward the Jewish state. Instead, Hamas apologists suppress facts, invent narratives, and repackage outlandish neo-Marxist talking points.

On October 9, two days after the Hamas massacres, Rashid Khalidi, Edward Said professor of modern Arab studies at Columbia University, declared that the Israel-Hamas war must "be put within the context. And the context is not just occupation. The context is settler colonialism and apartheid."[1]

On October 19, in an "Open Letter from the Art Community to Cultural Organizations," more than 500 "artists, writers, curators, filmmakers, publishers and workers who produce work, collaborate and communicate" opined about the Israel-Hamas war. The letter's signatories prominently included photographer and activist Nan Goldin, who focuses on the LGBT world; UC Berkeley Professor Judith Butler, who specializes in comparative literature and critical theory; and Columbia University Professor Saidiya Hartman, whose research interests include African American and American literature and cultural history, as well as gender, sexuality, queer theory, and feminism. The art community denizens—who did not claim knowledge of military operations or international law, firsthand acquaintance with unfolding events, regional expertise, or understanding of Islam—accused Israel of perpetrating "escalating genocide" and declared that the war's "root cause" is "oppression" and "occupation."

In another October 19 letter, this one addressed to President Biden and again signed by Goldin and Butler, "a group of Jewish American writers, artists and academics" invoked their Judaism to pronounce authoritatively on the Israel-Hamas war. But they omitted any mention of their competence to discuss jihad, Middle East politics, or national security.

"We believe it is possible and in fact necessary to condemn Hamas's actions and acknowledge the historical and ongoing oppression of the Palestinians," the Jewish artists and intellectuals asserted. "We believe it is possible and necessary to condemn Hamas's attack and take a stand against the collective punishment of Gazans that is unfolding and accelerating as we write."

1 "Historian Rashid Khalidi: Palestinians 'Living under Incredible Oppression, . . . It Had to Explode,'" *Democracy Now!*, October 9, 2023, https://www.democracynow.org/2023/10/9/rashid_khalidi_palestine_israel_explosion.

The Jewish artists did not acknowledge, much less take a stand against, Hamas's determination to wipe out the Jewish state. Nor did they provide evidence that Israel's siege, which, in principle, is legal under the laws of war, constituted unlawful collective punishment.

On October 22, 69 professors and 595 students and alumni published in the *Daily Princetonian* an open letter "in solidarity with Gaza" addressed to university president Christopher Eisgruber. The professors, students, and alumni wrote "to express our unequivocal outrage over the tragic loss of Israeli and Palestinian lives during the past week" but suggested that Israel acting in self-defense was worse than Hamas jihadists butchering civilians.

While declining to describe Hamas's documented atrocities, they accused Israel of engaging in "the targeting of civilians by the relentless bombing of hospitals, homes, roads, schools, universities, and infrastructures of survival in the Gaza Strip" while imposing "unchecked collective punishment."

One of the links provided by the Princetonians falsely accuses Israel of bombing Al-Ahli Arab Hospital. None of the links provides evidence that Israel targets civilians, as opposed to striking legitimate military targets that Hamas has placed in densely populated civilian areas.

On October 24, at a UN Security Council meeting, UN Secretary-General António Guterres supplied more supposed context. "It is important to also recognize the attacks by Hamas did not happen in a vacuum," Guterres said. "The Palestinian people have been subjected to 56 years of suffocating occupation. They have seen their land steadily devoured by settlements and plagued by violence; their economy stifled; their people displaced and their homes demolished. Their hopes for a political solution to their plight have been vanishing."

Like the context-obscuring assertions by artists, professors, and students, the UN secretary-general's statement rests on falsehoods, dogma, and ideology.

Consider just a few crucial components of context obscured, suppressed, or denied by the Hamas apologists.

First, Gaza Palestinians have not been subject to 56 years of occupation (since the 1967 war). In September 2005 Israel withdrew from the Gaza Strip, removing every Israeli soldier and civilian and offering the Palestinian Authority a comprehensive plan for joining forces to reconstruct Gaza. Four months later, in January 2006, Hamas won Gaza's local legislative elections.

In June 2007 Hamas violently seized control of the entire territory, expelled the PA, and turned Gaza into an armed camp for launching war against the Jewish state. The source of Hamas's hostility is not Israel's security barrier. It's Israel's very existence. Hamas's plans—funded by the Islamic Republic of Iran, which shares Hamas's goal to annihilate the Jewish state—compelled Israel to fortify its Gaza border (Egypt maintains strict control over its Gaza border) and impose a blockade. If Gaza is, as the apologists like to declare, "an open-air prison," Hamas, not Israel, serves as the prison warden. Gaza's jihadist rulers have impoverished the Palestinians who live there by diverting massive resources from the people to produce rockets and missiles and to construct hundreds of miles of terror tunnels.

Second, Israel is not guilty of "colonialism." As columnist Chaim Levinson observed in the Israeli daily *Haaretz*, whereas colonialism involves a great power imposing its institutions on, and transporting its people to live in, foreign lands, the Jews of pre-1948 Palestine rebelled against the internationally authorized British rule over the territory. Professor Khalidi's appeal to the fashionable doctrine of "settler colonialism"—the intruder's displacement of an indigenous population—to describe Israel only magnifies the absurdity. If indigenousness is the standard, it's the jihadists who have committed settler colonialism: Jewish sovereignty in the land of Israel preceded the arrival of Muslim Arab tribes by more than 1,500 years.

Third, Israel is not an apartheid state. Apartheid was a legal system designed in the mid-twentieth century by South Africa's white minority that established racial segregation and institutionalized political and economic discrimination against the country's majority black population.

It slanders Israel to apply the label "apartheid" to either the situation of Israel's Arab citizens or that of Gaza or West Bank Palestinians.

Arab citizens, about 21 percent of Israel's population, enjoy full civil and political rights. That is not to deny that, like ethnic minorities in other liberal democracies, they confront social barriers and government neglect that hamper full participation in national life.

Since Gazan and West Bank Palestinians have never been Israeli citizens, apartheid also does not apply. Israel turned over Gaza to the territory's Palestinian residents in 2005. And while the Jewish state still maintains effective military control over Judea and Samaria, West Bank Palestinians exercise self-government to a considerable extent. But West Bank Palestinians' complex legal and political circumstances stem from a protracted dispute between the two peoples and not the subjugation of one group of citizens by other citizens.

Fourth, while Israel strives to operate within the parameters of the international laws of war, Hamas flagrantly violates them. Hamas has committed crimes against humanity both by intentionally slaughtering Israeli civilians and by deliberately conducting military operations from within its own civilian areas, which unlawfully transforms Palestinians into human shields. Whereas Hamas deliberately kills, maims, rapes, and kidnaps civilians, Israel tries to minimize harm to civilians—not least by dropping leaflets in Gaza that direct noncombatants to evacuate areas from which Hamas operates—as the Israel Defense Forces pursue the legitimate military objective of destroying Hamas's ability to wage war and govern.

Fifth, Hamas apologists must be motivated by something other than human decency and concern for the loss of life in the Middle East. Compare, for example, their vehement response to the Israel-Hamas war and their nonresponse to the Syrian civil war. Before October 7, in the approximately 100-year conflict between Jews and Arabs over the land between the Jordan River and the Mediterranean Sea, about 91,000 Arabs have perished[2], while the Israeli War of Independence created approximately 650,000 Palestinian refugees (and more than 800,000 Jewish refugees from Arab countries).[3]

The still-raging Syrian civil war, which broke out in 2011, has produced death and displacement on a vastly greater scale: It has taken between 350,000 and 614,000 lives, left 6.8 million people internally displaced, and produced 5.4 million Syrian refugees abroad.[4] Yet how many of the students, professors, artists, and UN officials who have been quick to denounce Israel's exercise of its right to self-defense have, over the last 12 years, decried, demonstrated against, and demanded an end to the carnage in Syria?

Responsible consideration of context indicates that those sincerely concerned for Gaza Palestinians should hope and pray that Israel swiftly achieves the declared aim of its just war of self-defense: Hamas's destruction as a military and governing power.

2 "Total Casualties, Arab-Israeli Conflict" Jewish Virtual Library, accessed November 1, 2023, https://www.jewishvirtuallibrary.org/total-casualties-arab-israeli-conflict.

3 "Myths & Facts—The Refugees," Jewish Virtual Library, accessed November 1, 2023, https://www.jewishvirtuallibrary.org/myths-and-facts-the-refugees.

4 "Syria Situation," UNHCR, accessed November 1, 2023, https://reporting.unhcr.org/operational/situations/syria-situation.

27

NETANYAHU'S "SAUDI ARABIA BIND" MUDDLES PLANNING FOR "THE DAY AFTER"

December 31, 2023

TEL AVIV—"Hamas must be destroyed, Gaza must be demilitarized, and Palestinian society must be deradicalized," maintained Israel Prime Minister Benjamin Netanyahu last week in a *Wall Street Journal* op-ed. "These are the three prerequisites for peace between Israel and its Palestinian neighbors in Gaza."

After Israel destroys Iran-backed Hamas, Netanyahu made clear, the Palestinian Authority, which is led by 88-year-old President Mahmoud Abbas and governs Palestinians living in Judea and Samaria, would have no role in demilitarizing Gaza or in removing the teaching of hatred and the preaching of terror from its schools. Furthermore, Netanyahu emphasized, "For the foreseeable future Israel will have to retain overriding security responsibility over Gaza." Netanyahu left unclear, however, the PA's role, if any, in governing the tiny, war-torn stretch of land, home to some 2.2 million Palestinians, the day after "Hamas is destroyed, Gaza is demilitarized and Palestinian society begins a deradicalization process."

One reason for his ambiguity on the distribution of responsibility in rebuilding and governing Gaza is Netanyahu's Saudi Arabia bind. Netanyahu has been keen to reach a formal agreement with Riyadh on normalizing relations to consolidate the gains of the 2020 Abraham Accords. But after his narrow victory in the November 2022 elections, he assembled a governing coalition whose extreme members would rather bring down the government than support measures promoting the Palestinian self-government necessary to seal a Saudi deal. Because of US interest in a stable Middle East, Netanyahu's Saudi Arabia bind is also America's Saudi Arabia bind.

The prime minister's Saudi Arabia bind came into focus early last year not long after his governing coalition took office in late December 2022. Two hardline religious ultranationalists essential to preserving Netanyahu's coalition—Treasury Minister and Minister in the Defense Ministry Bezalel Smotrich and National Security Minister Itamar Ben-Gvir—could be counted on to reject steps toward greater Palestinian prosperity and self-rule that Saudi Arabia had publicly indicated were a precondition for establishing official diplomatic relations with Israel.

Furthermore, the ill-conceived judicial overhaul that Justice Minister Yariv Levin announced one week after Netanyahu's government was sworn in weakened the prime minister's already weak prospects for a breakthrough with Riyadh. Controversy over the government's sweeping reform package, characterized by an impassioned opposition as "regime change," plunged Israel into a political crisis that consumed the nation until approximately 6:30 a.m. on October 7, when Hamas jihadists launched their savage rampage through Israel's Gaza-border communities.

Netanyahu's Saudi Arabia bind had reemerged in September in advance of the October 7 massacre, which Hamas probably timed to undermine efforts by Israel and Saudi Arabia to overcome their differences. Saudi Arabia Crown Prince and Prime Minister Mohammed bin Salman had let it be known that in pursuit of an agreement with the

United States to improve security cooperation between the two nations—the principal threat coming from the Islamic Republic of Iran, the chief sponsor of not only Hamas, but also of Iran-backed Hezbollah—the kingdom also sought a normalization accord with Israel. To move forward, bin Salman stipulated, Israel would need to take tangible steps to show commitment to the establishment of a Palestinian state. Ministers Smotrich and Ben-Gvir, however, remained both daunting obstacles to compromise and essential components of Netanyahu's coalition.

The Israel-Hamas war has produced a third iteration of Netanyahu's Saudi Arabia bind. Instead of poisoning Israel's relations with the Muslim world as the jihadists hoped, Hamas's savage attack persuaded Saudi Arabia, along with the United Arab Emirates, Egypt, and others—though they won't say this out loud—that Israel must destroy Hamas as a fighting force and governing organization.

At the same time, according to several Israelis familiar with Riyadh's thinking, Saudi Arabia is prepared to provide substantial financial assistance to reconstruct Gaza. The Saudis, however, have attached two conditions: First, Israel must demonstrate willingness to advance the establishment of a Palestinian state. Second, Israel must accept the PA as the ruling power in Gaza. So stated, it is harder to imagine Smotrich and Ben-Gvir acquiescing to these terms than the ones the Saudis set for normalization.

The Biden administration—which, to its great credit, has ensured that Israel receives the munitions necessary to wage war against Hamas and defended Israel against denunciation in the United Nations—has doubled down on its support for a Palestinian state encompassing West Bank and Gazan Palestinians. In early November, at the G7 Foreign Ministers meeting in Tokyo, Secretary of State Antony Blinken stressed that "sustained peace between Israel and the Palestinians must include the Palestinian people's voices and aspirations at the center of post-crisis governance in Gaza," as well as "Palestinian-led governance and Gaza unified with the West Bank under the Palestinian Authority." Less than two weeks later, in a *Washington Post* op-ed, President Biden stated, "We stand firmly with the Israeli people as they defend themselves against the murderous nihilism of Hamas" while insisting that "[t]he Palestinian people deserve a state of their own and a future free from Hamas."

During his mid-December visit to Israel, National Security Advisor Jake Sullivan introduced a crucial qualification to the administration's backing of the PA and a Palestinian state. "Ultimately, governance of the West Bank and Gaza needs to be connected," Sullivan asserted. "And it needs to be connected under a revamped and revitalized Palestinian Authority."

Sullivan's refinement of the Biden administration position—the PA that "ultimately" governs Palestinians in Judea and Samaria and which will return to Gaza must be "revamped and revitalized"—is crucial because the PA that exists today is weak and corrupt. It also lacks legitimacy: If the PA had deigned to hold an election for president since Abbas's term expired in 2009, Hamas probably would have won. The PA counters Hamas and maintains power in the West Bank thanks to substantial security assistance from the Israel Defense Forces and the Israeli Security Agency.

The best that might be said about the PA's playing a key role in the reconstruction and governing of Gaza—and it is decisive—is that the alternatives are worse. An international coalition is bound to be unmotivated, incompetent, and toothless. Israeli rule would place the Jewish state back where it was in 2005 before it evacuated Gaza—governing a people who bitterly resent it, only this time the population has almost doubled, and many among them will seek to exact revenge for the devastation wrought by the current war. *New York Times* columnist Thomas Friedman's frivolous suggestion earlier this month that Israel should simply exit Gaza and let Hamas leader Yahya Sinwar pay the price for picking up the pieces is a recipe for bloody chaos on Israel's border.

While Netanyahu has not presented the public a plan for the day after, other than a commitment to demilitarization and deradicalization after defeat of Hamas on the battlefield, a widespread consensus prevails within the Israeli security establishment and among the citizenry that Israel must retain overall security control of Gaza for the indefinite future. While the security establishment also generally believes that Palestinians connected in one way or the other to the PA must take part in reconstructing and governing Gaza, the public appears to be less persuaded. The political leadership has done little to persuade them.

As Shmuel Rosner argues in his weekend column in the Hebrew-language daily *Maariv*, a version of which was translated in the *Jewish Journal*, neither Netanyahu nor other senior officials have told a traumatized public the hard truth: "Israel has no convincing alternative to the Palestinian Authority." The best available plan resembles, maintains Rosner, "what has been going on for many years, with varying degrees of success, in Judea and Samaria. In other words: control by the PA, and freedom of action for the IDF." This is not "a perfect solution," Rosner recognizes, but it is "a realistic, tolerable one."

This highly imperfect option, whose principal merit is that it is less flawed than the others, can be reconciled "ultimately" with US National Security Advisor Sullivan's call for a "revamped and revitalized" PA. Such a reconciliation might also enable Netanyahu to extricate himself and the United States from their Saudi Arabia bind by meeting Riyadh's demands without provoking Smotrich and Ben-Gvir to topple the government. Netanyahu need only employ his vaunted rhetorical skills to define a revamped and revitalized PA as one that ultimately meets the conditions that he specified in his 2009 Bar Ilan speech for establishing a Palestinian state: The PA must recognize Israel as the nation-state of the Jewish people and accept the demilitarization of its own state-to-be.

By reaffirming his own baseline for establishing a Palestinian state in the long term, Netanyahu would enable Israel to take advantage of Saudi financial support and American diplomatic support in the short and immediate term. He would also act on a principle that guides the best security thinking in the Jewish state: Israel should provide for the maximum Palestinian self-rule consistent with the fundamental requirements of Israeli national security.

28

HAMAS, THE PA, AND UNRWA EDUCATE GAZA SCHOOLCHILDREN FOR JIHAD

January 7, 2024

Gaza Strip schools fostered the depraved sensibility that fueled the October 7 butchery perpetrated by Iran-backed Hamas jihadists in southern Israel. While Hamas exercised dictatorial authority over the whole of jihadist indoctrination in Gaza, the Palestinian Authority produced the textbooks and lesson plans, and the United Nations Relief and Works Agency in significant measure administered the schools. The defeat of jihadism in Gaza will not be complete without a fundamental reorientation of its educational system.

Given US interests in Middle East stability, and the post-Israel-Hamas war reconstruction of Gaza in particular, American policymakers must grasp the extent of the preaching of hatred, violence, and Islamist supremacy woven into Gaza education. One obstacle is that many US diplomats, especially the younger career foreign service officers who staff them, will have been indoctrinated at American universities in opinions and ideas that bear an uncanny resemblance to certain ugly dogmas championed by the jihadists.

The Institute for Monitoring Peace and Cultural Tolerance in School Education (IMPACT-se) provides indispensable English-language documentation of the training for terrorism inscribed in UNRWA Arabic-language textbooks and other Hamas educational materials. The training falsifies history, encourages submission to Gaza's government-sanctioned doctrines, and fosters loathing of Jews, Israel, America, and the freedom and democracy central to the West. Hamas's brutal October 7 assault on Israel's border communities was not a hideous departure from the central tenets of Gazan education but rather gave faithful expression to them.

In "Al-Fateh—the Hamas Web Magazine for Children: Indoctrination to Jihad, Annihilation and Self-Destruction," IMPACT-se examined 145 of the Hamas publication's issues, from September 2002 to April 2009. *Al-Fateh*'s "consistent educational message to its young readers," according to IMPACT-se, "mirrors that of the Hamas movement's ideology and includes scathing hatred, disdain, delegitimization and demonization of the other—the West, especially the United States and Europe, the Jews, Israel and Zionism—as well as a call for establishing an Islamic state in entire Palestine and the annihilation of the State of Israel through violent liberation of the land in jihad."

Al-Fateh—in Arabic, "the Conqueror"—portrays "Jews as enemies of mankind and killers of prophets," IMPACT-se shows. Rejecting compromise, negotiations, and peace agreements—those in operation and the pursuit of new ones—*Al-Fateh* advocates "total commitment to an armed and violent jihad, especially of the suicidal kind." Through "its pervasive indoctrination of the younger generation into the cult of martyrdom," Al-Fateh contributed to forming "the next generation of suicide bombers to join the violent jihad."

Many October 7 jihadists—who murdered Israeli parents in front of their children and Israeli children in front of their parents; humiliated, maimed, and raped Jewish women; mutilated corpses; and kidnapped mostly civilians—and many Gaza Palestinians who cheered on the sadistic killers grew up on *Al-Fateh*'s poisonous tenets. They learned from the Hamas magazine that Israel and the United States, along with their friends and partners, are evil and implacable adversaries: "The Jewish enemy kills our people in beloved Palestine, while the United States, Britain and the other European countries, and India help it." They read that the United States is an omnipresent and insidious menace: "America is the terror, my child . . . she is the plague that destroys my liver . . . she is the viper that scatters poison inside me." And they were informed that Islam confronts a globe-spanning war: "Muslims and their children everywhere are under a siege of injustice—in beloved imprisoned Palestine, in wounded Afghanistan, in Kashmir, in Chechnya, and in other parts of the world which are controlled by the most despicable of God's creatures: the Jews, and their agents in crusader America."

In "Review of 2022 UNRWA-Produced Study Materials in the Palestinian Territories," IMPACT-se surveyed the curriculum overseen by UNRWA in West Bank and Jerusalem schools, as well as those in Gaza. Contrary to the UN charter and the Universal Declaration of Human Rights, which affirm basic rights and fundamental freedoms, UNRWA's Palestinian schools promulgate intolerance, conquest by force, and Islamic supremacy. UNRWA education features "a systematic insertion of violence, martyrdom, overt antisemitism, and *jihad* across all grades and subjects, with the proliferation of extreme nationalism and Islamist ideologies throughout the curriculum, including science and math textbooks; rejection of the possibility of peace with Israel; and the complete omission of any historical Jewish presence in the modern-day territories of Israel and the PA."

IMPACT-se released "UNRWA Education: Textbooks and Terror" in November 2023. In addition to detailing the praise that UNRWA staff members heaped on Hamas terrorists for the October 7 slaughter and the role played by UNRWA school graduates in the barbarities, the report examines UNRWA educational materials that "either harness antisemitism or encourage martyrdom or violent jihad."

For example, UNRWA teachers develop students' reading comprehension through a story that celebrates suicide bombers and the decapitation of Israeli soldiers. A map for fourth graders in UNRWA schools erases Israel by placing a Palestinian flag over all the land between the Jordan River and the Mediterranean Sea. A fifth-grade reading lesson, "Hooray for the Heroes," glorifies Palestinians "associated with war, violence, religious extremism, and Terrorism" but "does not include scientists, doctors, engineers, or athletes." UNRWA schools teach sixth-grade students that "[t]he Zionists are the terrorists of the modern age, and they are fated to disappear."

In addition, documents IMPACT-se, UNRWA teachers falsely instruct students that in Israel's 1948 War of Independence—five invading Arab armies sought to annihilate the newborn Jewish state—Zionists were compelled by Jewish religious belief to massacre Arabs. UNRWA school lessons disparage peaceful lives while glorifying martyrdom in the fight against infidels (most prominently Jews and Christians) as a noble act that Allah will reward in heaven. Gazan students learn that jihad to liberate Palestine is a "private obligation for every Muslim." That obligation applies to girls and women: "Palestinian girls are encouraged to kill, be killed, and send their children to die."

Israel's destruction of Hamas as a fighting force and governing authority in Gaza will provide at best temporary reprieve if, after major military operations end, the PA and UNRWA continue to propagate jihadism through the schools. The United States would be in a better position to assist in thwarting this abuse of UN institutions and Palestinian children if America's own educational system were not itself saturated with concepts that bear an alarming resemblance to those of jihadist indoctrination.

Although the US public only recently has taken serious notice of the problem, American colleges and universities have for many years promulgated as campus orthodoxy the multilayered accusation that the country is divided into white oppressors and oppressed people of color, that the American political system is racist to its core, and that social justice requires redistributing wealth and power by discriminating based on race. Institutions of higher education that have abandoned their mission, which is to transmit knowledge and cultivate independent thinking, in favor of the reproduction of hard-left ideology, cannot be expected to form diplomats capable of grasping the harms caused by the UN-sponsored Palestinian education for jihad or of possessing the judgment and motivation to implement the urgently needed correctives.

Here, as elsewhere, effective US foreign policy depends on thoroughly reforming higher education in America.

29

THE INTERNATIONAL COURT OF JUSTICE ON TRIAL

January 25, 2024

Yesterday, less than two weeks after the conclusion of its public hearings concerning the charge of genocide South Africa brought against Israel, the International Court of Justice (ICJ) in The Hague announced that it will issue an interim decision tomorrow. The ICJ will rule on whether to grant emergency measures to restrain Israel's military operations in Gaza. A final decision concerning the entirety of South Africa's complaint could take months or even years.

Nevertheless, with its impending judgment, the ICJ is on trial. If it fails to reject South Africa's scurrilous accusation, the ICJ should lose what legitimacy it possesses, at least among men and women around the world who respect facts, the rights of nation-states to defend themselves against barbaric aggression, and the rule of law.

In late December South Africa applied to initiate proceedings against the Jewish state. It demanded that Israel suspend military operations against Iran-backed Hamas on the grounds that the Jewish state was violating multiple provisions of the 1948 Genocide Convention.

South Africa filed its formal accusation of genocide fewer than three months after thousands of Hamas jihadists, under the cover of thousands of rockets fired at civilian areas, stormed through Israel's Gaza border communities, killing, raping, maiming, mutilating, and kidnapping as many civilians as they could find. South Africa's filing also came three-quarters of a century after Nazi Germany killed 6 million Jews in a systematic and unprecedented campaign of extermination that gave the crime of genocide its name.

International law knows of no graver crime than genocide. The 1948 convention, which Israel was among the first nations to join, defines genocide as the perpetration of any of several heinous crimes—killing members of a group, physically or mentally harming them, deliberately exposing them to fatal dangers, preventing their births, or forcibly transferring their children to another group—"with intent to destroy, in whole or in part, a national, ethnical, racial or religious group, as such."

Hamas's stated aim is genocide. The jihadists do not hide that they seek to destroy not only Israel but also global Jewry. Four years ago, for example, Hamas leader Fathi Hamad called on Palestinians around the world to eradicate the Jewish people: "Seven million Palestinians outside, enough warming up, you have Jews with you in every place. You should attack every Jew possible in all the world and kill them."[1]

At a January 3 press briefing, Biden administration National Security Council Spokesman John Kirby asserted that South Africa's genocide charges against Israel are "meritless, counterproductive, and completely without any basis in fact whatsoever."

Three initial considerations bolster the Biden administration's unequivocal assessment.

---

1 Agence France-Presse, "Hamas Official Condemned After Calling on Palestinians to Kill Jews," *Voice of America*, July 15, 2019, https://www.voanews.com/a/middle-east_hamas-official-condemned-after-calling-palestinians-kill-jews/6171870.html.

First, South Africa has long sympathized with Hamas, despite the jihadists' founding, and oft reaffirmed, commitment to extirpating Israel.[2] On October 7, the very day Hamas launched its massacre, the South African Ministry of International Relations and Cooperation issued a statement that sought to block Israel's exercise of its right of self-defense and blamed the Jewish state for Hamas's slaughter of Jews: "South Africa calls for the immediate cessation of violence, restraint, and peace between Israel and Palestine. South Africa expresses its grave concern over the recent devastating escalation in the Israeli-Palestinian conflict. The new conflagration has arisen from the continued illegal occupation of Palestine land, continued settlement expansion, desecration of the Al Aqsa Mosque and Christian holy sites, and ongoing oppression of the Palestinian people."

Second, the ICJ's composition weakens its capacity for impartial adjudication of Israel's defense against Hamas's ambitions to wipe it out. The court's bylaws call for its 15 judges to "be elected from among persons of high moral character, who possess the qualifications required in their respective countries for appointment to the highest judicial offices, or are jurisconsults of recognized competence in international law." But the qualifications for appointment to their highest judicial offices differ from country to country. In particular the qualifications in free and democratic nation-states differ from those in authoritarian regimes, as the qualifications in nation-states that protect religious liberty differ from those in countries that don't.

Currently, the court includes judges from the world's two most powerful authoritarian regimes: Russia and China. Vladimir Putin's Russia and Xi Jinping's China oblige judges to put the regime's interest in the nation's supremacy ahead of human rights and international law.

---

2 "Hamas Covenant 1988," Avalon Project, August 18, 1988, https://avalon.law.yale.edu/20th_century/hamas.asp.

Another factor determining a country's judicial qualifications is the relationship between religion and the state. Three of the ICJ judges are citizens of Muslim-majority countries that recognize Islam as an official state religion: Lebanon, Somalia, and Morocco. Leading interpretations of Islam place sharia law above human rights and international law.

Third, the neglect by the ICJ and member nations of war crimes and genocide elsewhere in the world erodes the court's claim to administer impartial justice. Last November, the ICJ issued its first ruling against Syria, requiring it to prevent torture. Why has it taken the court and member nations 12 years after the commencement of the Syrian War—which has killed hundreds of thousands, displaced 12 million people (more than half of the country's population), including at least 5 million refugees abroad—to address war crimes in Syria?

Since 2015, moreover, the Yemeni people have faced a massive humanitarian crisis. Why has the ICJ not heard complaints about violations of the laws of war and human rights in that long-standing conflict? And in January 2021, then-Secretary of State Mike Pompeo formally determined[3]—and his successor, Secretary of State Antony Blinken, subsequently reaffirmed[4]—that the internment of some 1 million Muslim Uyghurs by the Chinese Communist Party (CCP) in China's Xinjiang province, along with other forms of oppression against them, rose to the level of crimes against humanity and genocide. One would not know of the CCP's inhumanity from the ICJ's docket, however, which has not received a complaint against China brought by South Africa or, for that matter, any other member country.

In his somber January 12 opening argument, Israeli Ministry of Foreign Affairs Legal Advisor Tal Becker made a compelling prima facie case

3 "Determination of the Secretary of State on Atrocities in Xinjiang," United States Department of State, January 19, 2021, https://2017-2021.state.gov/determination-of-the-secretary-of-state-on-atrocities-in-xinjiang.

4 "Secretary Antony J. Blinken at a Press Availability," United States Department of State, January 27, 2021, https://www.state.gov/secretary-antony-j-blinken-at-a-press-availability.

that South Africa's allegations were meritless. "The Applicant has regrettably put before the Court a profoundly distorted factual and legal picture," Becker stated. "The entirety of its case hinges on a deliberately curated, decontextualized, and manipulative description of the reality of current hostilities."

South Africa's warping of facts and law, according to Becker, comprised several elements. South Africa delegitimized Israel as the nation-state of the Jewish people, assigned virtually all blame for the Israeli-Palestinian conflict to Israel, suppressed Hamas's responsibility for Gaza poverty, and obscured the Israeli victims' humanity.

Becker acknowledged the tragedy of Palestinian civilians' suffering "in a war" that Israel "did not start and did not want" and "in which Israel is defending itself against Hamas, Palestinian Islamic Jihad, and other terrorist organizations whose brutality knows no bounds."

Nevertheless, he argued, "as this Court has already made clear, the Genocide Convention was not designed to address the brutal impact of intensive hostilities on the civilian population, even when the use of force raises 'very serious issues of international law' and involves 'enormous suffering' and 'continuing loss of life.'" Whereas the Genocide Convention criminalizes acts aimed at destroying a people, Israel's military campaign, as government officials have made clear, intends to destroy Hamas, a military force that seeks Israel's destruction.

Hamas's flagrant violations of the laws of war do not absolve Israel of the obligation to adhere to the laws of war, but Hamas's war crimes do affect the application of Israel's obligations to the Gaza fighting. Hamas's unlawful war aim is the annihilation of Israel. To this end, Hamas unlawfully targets, terrorizes, and kills Israeli citizens. Hamas unlawfully kidnaps Israeli civilians and unlawfully uses them and Palestinian noncombatants as human shields. And Hamas unlawfully employs civilian infrastructure to wage war and unlawfully constructs tunnels for military use under civilian areas. One aim of Hamas's unlawful acts is to force Israel—even as the Jewish state seeks, consistent with the laws of war, to minimize civilian casualties and damage to civilian infrastructure—to cause terrifying levels of death and destruction in Gaza.

It cannot be said enough, but it is hardly said at all: While Israel remains bound by the international laws of war, Hamas is morally and legally responsible for the Gaza carnage because of its fiendish strategic decision, as part of its decades-long campaign to eliminate Israel, to transform Gaza's urban areas into battlefields.

Becker asked the ICJ to keep in mind three crucial points obscured by South Africa's accusations.

First, it is particularly ugly and perverse to bring false charges of genocide against Israel given Hamas's "proudly declared agenda of annihilation, which is not a secret, and is not in doubt."

Second, under the international laws of war, "Israel has the inherent right to take all legitimate measures to defend its citizens and secure the release of the hostages."

Third, it is the complainant South Africa that should be directed by the ICJ to take remedial action because of its close relations over many years with an organization whose very reason for existence is, in defiance of the Genocide Convention, to destroy Israel. "It seems fitting, then," asserted Becker, "that [South Africa] be instructed to comply with those obligations itself; to end its own language of de-legitimization of Israel's existence; end its support for Hamas; and to use its influence with this organization so that Hamas permanently ends its campaign of genocidal terror and releases the hostages."

If, on Friday, the ICJ rejects South Africa's vile accusation, justice will have been served. If the ICJ sides with South Africa and finds, contrary to the facts and the law, that Israel must pare back its military operations out of a concern that it is engaging in genocide, then the ICJ will have usefully exposed itself as an international court of injustice.

30

ISRAEL'S REASONABLE WAR AIMS AND STRATEGY

February 25, 2024, discussing "The Goals of the War in Gaza—and the Strategy for Achieving Them" by Azar Gat

In "The Goals of the War in Gaza—and the Strategy for Achieving Them," published by the Institute for National Security Studies in Tel Aviv, my friend Azar Gat provides an excellent guide to Israel's internal national security debate. A Tel Aviv University political science professor and military-history scholar, Gat sketches in unadorned terms Israel's war aims and strategy. He also briskly evaluates the major doubts about the government's plans and the leading alternatives. His compelling conclusion is that Israel's principal objectives—destruction of Iran-backed Hamas's military and governmental capabilities and liberation of the hostages—"are vital and can be achieved simultaneously." Gat can insist on the unity of Israel's goals because he understands them in context and tempers expectations in light of the harsh realities of Middle East politics and of Gaza in particular.

On October 7, with Hamas jihadists attacking Israel's southern border communities and perpetrating horrific war crimes, Prime Minister

Benjamin Netanyahu proclaimed that Israel was at war. This reflected a decisive change in the Jewish state's strategic orientation.

Since Hamas's violent 2007 ouster of the Palestinian Authority from Gaza, the terrorist organization's periodic rocket bombardments of Israeli civilians and civilian infrastructure prompted Israel to undertake several military incursions into Gaza to degrade Hamas's capabilities and restore quiet. The jihadists' October 7 savagery shattered the comforting illusion—shared by Israel's governing coalition and opposition, military experts, and people—that the Jewish state could live with Hamas ruling Gaza. To eliminate Hamas's capacity to govern and wage war, Netanyahu's war cabinet, joined by the opposition's two most experienced national security figures, prepared a major ground offensive.

Initial domestic skepticism focused on the Israel Defense Forces' ability to maneuver in Gaza's tightly packed urban areas. Yet, writes Gat, "it has become clear, and not only to the surprise of the skeptics, that the IDF—both regular and reserve forces—is functioning at an extraordinary level through tight coordination, which may be unsurpassed by any other army in the world, among ground forces and the air force combined with other combat units and intelligence capabilities."

Hamas's ruthlessness and readiness provoked more skepticism. In flagrant violation of the international laws of war, the jihadists embedded their forces in cities. Only after the fighting had begun did Israel discover the intricacy, sophistication, and extent of the hundreds of miles of tunnels Hamas built under Gaza's civilian population and the enormous quantity of munitions and other military equipment the terrorist organization had amassed. "Nevertheless, the IDF gained control over Gaza City and the northern Strip and broke the organized defense of Hamas' battalions and its brigades in the field," reports Gat, "and the IDF is close to a similar achievement—despite challenging conditions and the spreading public despondency in relation to the perceived 'treading water'—in Khan Yunis."

While Palestinian casualties have been staggering owing to Hamas's conversion of urban areas into battlefields, Israel's successes have come with far fewer fallen Israeli soldiers—under 235 at midmonth, when Gat's analysis was published—than expected.

Critics in Israel have advocated several alternatives to Israel's ground campaign. Gat finds none of them persuasive.

Some proposed a comprehensive siege of Gaza that would within weeks or perhaps months compel Hamas to surrender or provoke Palestinians to topple the terrorists. However, Gat argues, "[T]he world and in particular the United States will not allow the starvation of 'the state of Gaza.'" Furthermore, to expect that "the people of Gaza could rise up and overthrow an organization as armed, fanatical, and determined as Hamas is no less a dream detached from reality."

Others have advocated for discrete, small-scale raids accompanied by air power targeting Hamas's infrastructure. Given the jihadists' substantial capabilities, Gat argues, surgical strikes without controlling territory would produce "an endless war of attrition, with the potential for no fewer casualties, a decline of Israeli morale, and a decisive moral victory for Hamas." That approach would also guarantee the continuation of Hamas's rocket fire while relinquishing the means to end it.

Still others want an immediate stop to the war. They maintain that Israel cannot achieve more than it already has, or it has achieved enough, and they generally favor aggressive efforts to secure a deal with Hamas to save the hostages.

Gat poses and answers a critical question: "What possible deal, as a practical matter, is on the table, and to what is it possible and necessary to agree?" Israel's war cabinet and a significant majority of the public are prepared to accept a ceasefire of a month or two in exchange for the hostages' release. A deal of this sort, he believes, could free dozens of the surviving elderly among the approximately 130 whom Hamas has not released. However, Gat emphasizes, Hamas has persisted in demanding "a ceasing of *the war*—not the fighting." That entails the IDF's withdrawal from Gaza, Hamas's return to power (even international guarantees of its wellbeing), and a captives deal of 'everyone for everyone,'" which would require Israel to release thousands of hardened jihadists.

Striking a deal "at any price," which means acquiescing to Hamas's outrageous conditions, would bring about a "crushing national defeat," states Gat. "It is necessary to make a supreme effort and be ready to pay a high price to rescue as many hostages as possible, but Israel's surrender on existential questions is not an option."

Such a surrender would reverberate to Israel's great detriment throughout the Middle East. "The Palestinians and Arab public opinion—inclined, in any case, to the 'axis of resistance'—would back Hamas," while "Israel's potential allies in the Arab Middle East would be compelled to silence themselves and draw back," maintains Gat. Hamas would reassert control, rearm, rebuild military infrastructure, and renew indiscriminate rocket attacks on Israeli civilian populations. Having sustained heartbreaking losses with nothing to show for it, Israel would be ill disposed to mobilize again for war against Hamas. And the United States would be decidedly less inclined to green-light another round of devastating urban warfare.

The biggest cost to Israel, emphasizes Gat, would be the destruction of its deterrence—that is, the perception that it can and will strike swiftly and decisively. At that point, with Hamas having proved itself able to survive a concerted Israeli offensive and willing to subject Gazans to massive collateral damage, what would deter Hamas in the future from attacking Israel? What would deter Hezbollah and other regional jihadists from redoubling their fortifications in towns and cities and stockpiling arms for deadlier assaults on Israel's civilian population?

Without the deterrence that has served as a cornerstone of the nation's strategic culture since the country's birth in 1948, Israel would lose the long periods of relative peace and quiet that have allowed it to build a flourishing society in a dangerous neighborhood. Instead, it would face a draining and debilitating multifront war against an array of Iran-backed Islamists seeking its destruction.

This constellation of costs, culminating with the withering of its deterrence, "is the source of the deep and justified feeling in Israel that the war in Gaza is an existential war," writes Gat.

"What is the 'victory' that Israel can realistically achieve in the war against Hamas," Gat asks, "and what apparently will not be possible to achieve?" Undistracted by Netanyahu's damaging political slogan of "absolute victory," Gat asserts that Israel can destroy Hamas's military leadership, fighting forces, and infrastructure and thwart its reemergence as Gaza's dominant power. This includes dismantling key nodes of Hamas's vast tunnel network—"munitions workshops, weapons and food stockpiles, and command and control centers"—along with the energy sources that power communications, lighting, and ventilation. Israel can also correct what Gat regards as the nation's only strategic error since October 7 by finally establishing control over the Philadelphi Corridor on Gaza's Egyptian border, through which Hamas has smuggled immense amounts of materials crucial to its military operations.

Hamas's total elimination, however, is not attainable. Following Israel's ground campaign, Gat argues, Hamas will continue to live in many Gazans' hearts. It will persist as a guerilla force. From time to time, the jihadists will launch volleys of rockets into Israel. But Israel will no longer be threatened by tens of thousands of entrenched jihadists possessing tens of thousands of rockets.

Unfortunately, battlefield success will not translate into a political solution for what ails Gaza. Despite its manifest flaws, the least awful option for "the day after" involves Israel maintaining overall security responsibility for Gaza. Moderate Gulf Arabs, the United States, and Europe must cooperate in reconstructing the war-torn territory. And Gaza should be administered by an "upgraded Palestinian Authority" that, like the PA in Judea and Samaria, enables Israeli forces to maneuver adroitly as needed against Hamas terrorists.

This astringent conclusion is not for want of imagination or empathy. To the contrary, it takes seriously local hearts and minds and reckons with the region's baleful geopolitical exigencies. In the Middle East, writes Gat, "there exist only bad options and much worse ones."

What is true of the Middle East is especially true of Gaza.

31

RECONCILING ISRAELI AND US PLANS FOR "THE DAY AFTER" IN GAZA

March 3, 2024

TEL AVIV—The United States and Israel have advanced apparently conflicting visions of the day after Israel defeats Iran-backed Hamas in Gaza. Whereas the Biden administration seeks the establishment of a Palestinian state, Israeli Prime Minister Benjamin Netanyahu's government plans on retaining overall security responsibility for Gaza and installing local Palestinian officials untainted to the degree possible by ties to terrorist organizations to administer civil affairs.

The neglected common ground between Israel and the United States offers an opportunity to make the terrible situation in Gaza less terrible.

On October 6, 2023, no one was talking about a two-state solution. Israel was mired in a social and political crisis triggered by the Netanyahu government's January 2023 proposal for a major overhaul of the Israeli judiciary. The Abraham Accords were facilitating growing security cooperation, commercial relations, and cultural exchange between the original parties—Israel, Bahrain, and the United Arab Emirates. In the face of the

Iran threat, the Biden administration was making progress toward a comprehensive deal with Saudi Arabia that would include normalization of relations with Israel if Jerusalem took steps to advance Palestinian independence. And Hamas, it was widely thought, in accordance with Netanyahu's stated policy of providing financial support for the terrorist organization, was content to sporadically fire rockets at Israel while gradually giving more attention to improving Gazans' economic wellbeing.

Yet in late October 2023, just a few weeks after Hamas's barbaric October 7 assault on Israel—during which the jihadists slaughtered around 1,200 mostly civilians, raped women, mutilated bodies, and kidnapped approximately 250, mostly civilians—President Joe Biden affirmed that the solution to the Israeli-Palestinian conflict required the creation of a Palestinian state.[1] That during periods of relative calm, Presidents Clinton, Bush, Obama, and Trump failed to midwife the birth of a Palestinian state did not seem to disturb Biden administration calculations.

The administration's push for a Palestinian state also appeared to disregard Israel's domestic politics. Despite the remarkable rallying of civil society in Israel to defend the nation, the Jewish state remained deeply divided. The trauma inflicted by the October 7 atrocities ran deep within Israelis, who were already reeling from the bruising battles over judicial reform, which had followed five destabilizing elections in three and a half years. And the country was engaged in a multifront war with Iran-backed militias. That included preparations for a full-scale ground campaign in Gaza, regarded by many Israelis as essential to the Jewish state's survival, and the suppression of daily rocket fire from Hezbollah in Lebanon on Israel's northern border. In those tense circumstances, and with the Palestinian Authority widely seen as corrupt and sclerotic, few

1 Barak Ravid, "Biden's Post-War Plan: Talks on a Two-State Solution to Israeli-Palestinian Conflict," Axios, October 26, 2023, https://www.axios.com/2023/10/26/biden-post-war-plan-two-state-solution-israel-palestinians.

Israelis were prepared to entertain yet another round of talks about a two-state solution.

Nevertheless, in a mid-December visit to the region while the Gaza war raged, National Security Advisor Jake Sullivan pressed for a PA-led Palestinian state. Before meeting in Ramallah with PA President Mahmoud Abbas, Sullivan said discussions would deal with efforts to "revamp and revitalize the Palestinian Authority."[2] At the meeting Sullivan "reemphasized President Biden's longstanding vision for a more peaceful, integrated, and prosperous Middle East region, and ultimately a path to a two-state solution that provides for equal measures of justice, freedom, and dignity for Israelis and Palestinians alike."[3]

It has been insufficiently observed that Sullivan left open the criteria that would guide the PA's revamping and revitalizing while highlighting "a path to a two-state solution" rather than the solution itself.

In late January 2024, *New York Times* columnist Thomas Friedman reported that the administration's ideas about the Middle East had crystalized into "a Biden doctrine." One track involved a tougher stance toward Iran. Another focused on tighter security cooperation with Saudi Arabia. A third called for "an unprecedented US diplomatic initiative to promote a Palestinian state—NOW," wrote Friedman. It was easy to overlook that Friedman's "NOW" referred not to the achievement of a Palestinian state but to its promotion.

Friedman identified demanding conditions that a Palestinian state must meet. The Biden doctrine's implementation, he argued, "would involve some form of US recognition of a demilitarized Palestinian state in the West Bank and Gaza Strip that would come into being only once

2 Victoria Kim and Aaron Boxerman, "Sullivan Says Both the US and Israel Expect Fighting to Slow Down Eventually," *New York Times*, December 15, 2023, https://www.nytimes.com/2023/12/15/world/middleeast/jake-sullivan-will-meet-israels-president-as-the-allies-diverge-on-war-strategy.html.

3 "Readout of National Security Advisor Jake Sullivan's Meetings with Palestinian Authority President Mahmoud Abbas," White House, December 15, 2023, https://www.whitehouse.gov/briefing-room/statements-releases/2023/12/15/readout-of-national-security-advisor-jake-sullivans-meetings-with-palestinian-authority-president-mahmoud-abbas.

Palestinians had developed a set of defined, credible institutions and security capabilities to ensure that this state was viable and that it could never threaten Israel."

In mid-February, Martin Indyk, who played a leading role in the unsuccessful efforts of Presidents Clinton and Obama to create a Palestinian state, echoed Sullivan's and Friedman's language. In "The Strange Resurrection of the Two-State Solution," published online at *Foreign Affairs* in late February, he argued that a Palestinian state is urgently needed. "There is no credible way to bring the war in Gaza to an end without trying to fashion a new, more stable order there," Indyk wrote. "But that cannot be done without also establishing a credible path to a two-state solution." Like Sullivan and Friedman, Indyk identified the ultimate destination but stressed the need to devise a plausible route.

Indyk observed, moreover, that several principal players in rebuilding Gaza are focused less on consummating the enterprise than on launching it properly while keeping in mind the overall target. "The Sunni Arab states, led by Saudi Arabia, are insisting on that as a condition for their support for the revitalization of the PA and the reconstruction of Gaza, as is the rest of the international community," he wrote. "The PA would need to be able to point to that goal in order to legitimize any role it played in controlling Gaza. And the Biden administration must be able to include the goal of two states as part of the Israeli-Saudi agreement it is still eager to broker."

One principal player, however, seems to have opted out of pursuit of a two-state solution. In late February, Prime Minister Netanyahu presented Israel's war cabinet with his long-awaited plan for the day after Israel's defeat of Hamas. In a one-page document, he enumerated principles to guide Israeli policy in Gaza for the short run, the intermediate run, and the long run. In line with much of Israeli public opinion, a Palestinian state was mentioned, only to reject its unilateral recognition.

In the short run, according to Netanyahu's statement of principles, Israel must destroy the jihadists' ability to govern and wage war, secure the hostages' return, and establish long-term protection against future threats from Gaza.

In the intermediate run, the document calls on Israel to address security imperatives and civilian administration. Israel must demilitarize Gaza, operate militarily throughout the territory, establish a security zone within Gaza on the Israel border, guard Gaza's border with Egypt while cooperating with Cairo and Washington to prevent smuggling into Gaza from the Sinai Peninsula, and exercise security control over the entire territory west of the Jordan River, which includes not only Israel and Gaza but also Judea and Samaria—home to West Bank Palestinians. Israel must also, to the extent possible, transfer administrative power to local Palestinians who have not trafficked in terrorism; deradicalize, in cooperation with Arab states, Gaza's religious, educational, and welfare institutions; close and replace UNRWA, the UN organization whose workers were involved in the October 7 attacks and whose schools teach jihadism; and following demilitarization and the commencement of deradicalization, help rebuild Gaza with the financial and administrative aid of Israel's friends and partners.

In the long run, a final-status agreement between Israel and the Palestinians "will only be achieved through direct negotiations between the sides without preexisting conditions." Furthermore, "Israel will continue to oppose unilateral recognition of a Palestinian state," the Netanyahu document states. "Such recognition following the Oct. 7 slaughter would grant a great prize without precedent to terror and would thwart any future peace arrangements."

Writing in *Tablet* in early February, Elliott Abrams, deputy national security advisor with responsibility for the Middle East for President George W. Bush, supplied additional reasons why, in the aftermath of the October 7 attacks, Israelis generally reject the establishment of a Palestinian state. In "The Two-State Delusion," he argued that proponents—true of Sullivan, Friedman, and Indyk—give little reason to believe that Israel and the Palestinian Authority are better situated today to resolve the vexing issues that have derailed decades of assiduous US efforts to reach a final-status agreement: the drawing of borders, the status of Jerusalem, and the plight of Palestinian refugees. In addition, warns Abrams, a Palestinian state in current circumstances is, to put matters gently, unlikely to respect individual freedom, democracy, and the rule of law. And it would provide Iran, the world's leading state sponsor of terror, a comfortable outpost on Israel's doorstep.

Nevertheless, even Netanyahu's statement of principles opposed not a Palestinian state but its "unilateral recognition." And not forever but as a reward for Hamas's mass atrocities. At the same time, Abrams's analysis sets forth practical criteria for Israel's recognition of a demilitarized Palestinian state at some point down the road: negotiated agreement on borders, Jerusalem, and refugees, coupled with viable political institutions and arrangements that provide for Israel's national security interests.

Building on the common ground between the Biden administration, Israel, and the Saudis and other Arab partners depends then on distinguishing between the long-term goal and salutary short- and intermediate-term undertakings. With the benefit of deft diplomacy and rhetorical fine-tuning, the parties can agree on the ambitious long-term goal, perhaps very long term, of a demilitarized Palestinian state. At the same time, they can jointly pursue short-term measures to defeat Hamas, return the hostages, provide humanitarian relief, deradicalize Gaza, install suitable civil administrators, and ensure overall Israeli responsibility for combatting the resurgence of jihadism along its southwestern border. Such vital short-term and intermediate-term measures are indispensable prerequisites for the establishment of a Palestinian state and the provision for Israel's security in the long term.

32

THE PUBLIC INTEREST FELLOWSHIP IN ISRAEL

March 17, 2024

TEL AVIV—Israel has always presented amazing contrasts. On its just-concluded 10-day trip to the Jewish state, amid Israel's war against Iran-backed Hamas in Gaza and the nation's low-intensity fighting against Iran-backed Hezbollah along the Lebanon border, The Public Interest Fellowship (TPIF) fellows and staff found the familiar contrasts on full display—and wrenching new ones, too.

With a population of approximately 9.3 million, including around 2.1 million Arab citizens, the nation-state of the Jewish people is the only rights-protecting democracy in a region—the Middle East and North Africa—of more than 500 million Muslims. Despite its diminutive size, youth, and the daunting security threats to which it has been constantly subject from the instant that David Ben-Gurion read aloud the country's Declaration of Independence in Tel Aviv on May 14, 1948, Israel has built the region's most advanced high-tech economy, most formidable and sophisticated military, and most robust civil society. And Israel has fostered an extraordinary diversity of Jews: of European, Middle Eastern, and North African descent; secular, traditional, and religious; and farmers and entrepreneurs, teachers and soldiers, scholars and chefs, artisans and contractors, warriors and winemakers, lawyers and doctors and business executives, social justice activists and hit TV show makers, small business owners and, yes—peoples and nations being what they are—thugs and criminal families.

Five months after some 3,000 Hamas jihadists invaded southern Israel to perpetrate mass atrocities against the nation's civilian population, new contrasts sear the Israeli psyche. In the face of the terrible national trauma inflicted by the jihadists on October 7, Israelis have shown remarkable resiliency. War has brought them together, but it has not dissipated the grievances, resentments, and enmities that fueled and were fueled by the preceding nine months of controversy over the government's proposed judicial overhaul. Not least, many with whom we spoke stressed the discrepancy between the people's heroic response to Hamas's bloodthirsty assault and the governing class's multiple failures to protect the nation.

TPIF prepares fellows to explore such complex political realities. Under the leadership of Executive Director Garrett Exner, Deputy Director Serena Frechter, and Director of Operations Nani Beraha, the program brings annually 10 or so talented young men and women to the nation's capital for two-year stints to do work—in journalism, with political consulting firms and public policy think thanks, at not-for-profit initiatives, and in Congress—that advances individual liberty, equality under law, limited government, free markets, vigorous civil society, and a strong America abroad. As the program's director of studies, I conduct bimonthly seminars on the modern tradition of freedom; host monthly dinners with distinguished figures from politics, national security, law, and journalism; and convene seasonal weekend retreats that allow fellows to delve into enduring ideas and contemporary issues. Every other year TPIF fellows and staff travel to Israel to improve our understanding of America's best friend and partner in the region.

On this trip, TPIF's fifth to Israel, the war forced adjustments to our itinerary. We spent several days in Tel Aviv and in Jerusalem; traveled through parts of Judea and Samaria; visited Rahat, a Bedouin city in the Negev; and picked garlic and weeded onion fields near Gaza. Security considerations compelled us to forgo our usual stops in Ramallah to meet with Palestinian Authority representatives, in the Golan Heights to observe the border with Syria, and in the upper Galilee within eyesight of Lebanon.

As on TPIF's previous Israel trips, we met a variety of speakers. We talked to journalists, former politicians and government officials, and active duty military officers. We heard from men and women of the left, center, and right. We spoke with a distinguished Arab-Israeli journalist and an eminent ultra-Orthodox rabbi. We listened to a traditionally garbed Bedouin woman—a mother of six and an entrepreneur who had launched a line of cosmetics—and to a 29-year-old woman who survived the Nova music festival massacre where Hamas gunned down more than 400 people and kidnapped more than 40. We engaged in discussions with Israelis who wished to expand Israel's presence in and control over Judea and Samaria, home to between 2.5 million and 3 million noncitizen West Bank Palestinians, and with Israelis who oppose such expansion and seek separation from the West Bank. We held conversations with prominent defenders of the Netanyahu government's judicial-reform efforts and its conduct of the Gaza war and of wartime diplomacy, and with prominent opponents of every aspect of the Netanyahu government.

We also participated in difficult but essential conversations with members of communities that Hamas had devastated. On October 7, the terrorists abducted Thomas Hand's then-eight-year-old daughter Emily from Kibbutz Be'eri. She was released as part of the November ceasefire. Pausing occasionally to collect himself, Emily's father told us with tears of wonderment that his daughter had already recovered to 95 percent of her old self.

Chen Kotler hosted us at Kfar Aza, another kibbutz on the Gaza border that Hamas invaded on October 7. While we sat on her porch, our guide, who just returned from nearly five months of reserve duty in the north, determined that the explosions in the distance were outgoing Israeli artillery fire.

Chen showed us where the jihadists burst through the kibbutz's back fence, about a mile from Gaza; rampaged through the young adults' quarters; and with advance knowledge of the kibbutz layout, clambered atop her roof, which overlooked the kibbutz armory, to ambush members rushing to obtain weapons. On that awful day, Hamas slaughtered 62 Kfar Aza kibbutzniks and abducted 19, five of whom the terrorists still hold hostage.

The war was the fixed point around which our conversations revolved. Israelis are a legendarily contentious people—try to agree, and as often as not, you will be informed with a wry smile that you don't—but those we encountered unanimously affirmed that the war marks a turning point in the nation's short history.

Here, too, we encountered a stunning contrast. Many Israelis share Amir Tibon's assessment. A journalist who, with his family, survived the jihadists' invasion of Kibbutz Nahal Oz, Tibon told us that the response to the October 7 attacks has been Israeli society's finest hour while exposing a dysfunctional governing class and public sector.

The intelligence community did not effectively warn of the murder and mayhem. The security barrier, designed to stop individuals and small groups of terrorists, was swiftly overwhelmed by thousands of jihadists who disabled its cameras and censors and cut through it or knocked it down, flew over it, or bypassed it by sea. In addition the military was caught unprepared: Too few troops were stationed on the border, and of those, too few stood ready to repel an attack. Most consequentially, the government's strategy for containing and deterring Hamas failed. Several years ago Prime Minister Benjamin Netanyahu authorized the delivery of tens of millions of dollars in cash a month to Hamas, courtesy of the Qatari government. Netanyahu aimed to divide West Bank Palestinians ruled by the PA from Gaza Palestinians controlled by Hamas while turning Hamas toward economic development. Instead, the Israel-supervised delivery of Qatari cash helped fund Hamas's massive tunnel infrastructure, enormous weapons stockpiles, and monstrous plans to destroy Israel.

At the same time, Israelis have shown breathtaking valor and unity. Some 350,000 reservists reported for duty within five days of the October 7 attacks. The Israel Defense Forces have made substantial progress toward destroying Hamas as a governing power and military while defying all expectations in minimizing casualties among comrades and among noncombatant Palestinians. In the war's early weeks, Israeli restaurant owners made available their kitchens for fellow citizens who set aside their regular jobs to prepare meals for the soldiers. Israelis from all walks of life travel to the north and south to work in the fields. Many Israelis have raised money to purchase essential equipment from abroad for frontline soldiers: helmets, protective vests, high-tech goggles, and more. And civil society has rallied to provide mental-health care and education for the tens of thousands of internally displaced citizens.

At Kfar Aza, Chen Kotler sent TPIF on its way with her own contrast, at once heartbreaking and fortifying, somber and hopeful. She stood in front of the kibbutz gate through which the jihadists stormed on that awful early autumn morning. Behind her lay Kfar Aza's green fields—sand and stone until the kibbutz, forgive the cliché, made the desert bloom. To the west, just beyond the spring crops, we could see Gaza—an easy walk and only a few minutes by motorcycle, pickup truck, or paraglider.

As Chen spoke, her quietly resolute voice occasionally faltered. We barely breathed. Her features taut and her tone grim, Chen told us that the war with Hamas is not just the kibbutz's war. It's not just Israel's war. It's not just the Jewish people's war. The war against Hamas is civilization's war, she said. And we must win it.

Then with a soft smile tinged with indelible sorrow, she told us that she believes in *shalom*—peace—which in Hebrew signifies, beyond the absence of fighting, the achievement of harmony in a broken world. We Israelis seek *shalom*, she concluded, because we love life.

We thanked Chen for her courage and told her that we would remember her words and share them with others.

33

RECLAIMING ISRAEL'S HYBRID CHARACTER

March 31, 2024, discussing The Eighth Day: Israel After October 7th *by Micah Goodman*

Israelis from all walks of life believe that Iran-backed Hamas's October 7 massacres changed something vital in them and in their country. The horrors of the recent past weigh on citizens' hearts and minds. Complex military operations in the south against Hamas and in the north against Iran-backed Hezbollah—along with the threat of intensifying fighting in both arenas, as well as the prospect of battles to come elsewhere in the region amid Israel's multifront war with Iran—stir anxieties and fray nerves. And keenly aware of the nation's bitter internal divisions, the resurgence of antisemitism in the West, faltering international support, and deteriorating relations with the United States, Israelis fear for their nation's future.

At the same time, post–October 7 Israelis have demonstrated abiding pride in their country and have exhibited inspiring resilience in the face of mass atrocities the likes of which no nation under assault has ever before witnessed broadcast in real time on its television screens and smartphones. Within days of the jihadists' invasion, more than 300,000 reservists in a country of 9.3 million people reported for duty. Citizens of every description volunteered—to prepare and deliver meals for the swollen military ranks, to care for grieving families whose loved ones had been butchered or kidnapped, to provide mental health and educational services for hundreds of thousands of displaced residents along the southern and northern borders who had been relocated to hotels around the country, and to pick fruits and vegetables in neglected fields and orchards. Israelis discovered following the October 7 savagery a unity of purpose and dedication to the common good of which many in the Jewish state had not known they were still capable.

Plunged into a war widely seen in the country as posing an existential threat and occupied with countless acts of sacrifice, courage, and devotion, Israelis have had little opportunity to step back to consider the big picture. They have scarcely begun to delve into the origins of their post–October 7 plight or explore the sources of their heroism. Until, that is, the Hebrew-language publication last week of *The Eighth Day: Israel after October 7th*, by my friend Micah Goodman.

Goodman's new book aims to assist fellow Israelis who share his apprehension and perplexity. Extraordinary for its swift composition and publication, multilayered and pinpoint analysis, and wise counsel in a dark hour, the book illuminates the collision of forces that brought the nation to the "apocalypse" of October 7 and brings into focus resources within the Israeli character and the Jewish tradition for revitalizing the Jewish state. Already underway, an English translation will help apprehensive and perplexed friends of Israel around the world to understand better the depths of the Jewish state's distress and the wellsprings of its renewal.

A fellow at the Shalom Hartman Institute in Jerusalem, Goodman has published six Israeli bestsellers on an impressive range of subjects: Maimonides, Yehuda Halevi, Moses, the Israeli-Palestinian conflict, the mutual antipathy and the mutual dependence in Israel of the religious and the secular, and the digital revolution and Israeli political polarization.

His books display a rare gift for expressing in clear and concise language trenchant distinctions, essential tensions, arresting paradoxes, and sustaining syntheses.

The Eighth Day uses that gift to clarify Israel's "hybrid character," the reclaiming of which, Goodman contends, is crucial not only to the nation's flourishing but also to its survival. As memorialized in its Declaration of Independence, Israel was born a Jewish, rights-protecting, and democratic country. And so it must remain, argues Goodman. Rooted in the modern tradition of freedom, which embraces equality of rights under law, self-fulfillment, and the diversity of ways of being human, Israel is also grounded in an ancient tradition, religious and national, that stresses family, community, and peoplehood.

On October 7, jihadists poured across Israel's border with Gaza to inflict evils of a kind that Jews had suffered during two millennia of exile and dispersion, but which Israel's founding was meant to end. The disaster confronted Israelis with a shattering discovery—or rediscovery: Notwithstanding the last 20 years of unprecedented growth and prosperity, they live in a dangerous neighborhood in which their existence is fragile and their survival is not guaranteed.

The invasion and the slaughter, according to Goodman, overturned two essential achievements of Zionism: the separation of Jews in time from a past of weakness and persecution, and the separation of Jews in place from homelessness and lack of sovereign control over their homes and land. October 7's devastating implication was that even with political power, Jews remain vulnerable to pogroms.

The catastrophe, however, did not refute Zionism. A tragic view of the world, inscribed in biblical faith, was familiar to Zionism's founding fathers. The refounding of their nation to which he summons Israelis represents, for Goodman, a return to and deepening of Zionism.

Goodman finds a key to "Israel's hidden architecture" in the relationship between the argument over judicial reform—which quickly deteriorated into an ugly dispute over the shape of the regime and the character of the Jewish state—that roiled the nation from January 4, 2023, to October 6, 2023, and the October 7 outbreak of war. The vehement debate over the proposed judicial system overhaul weakened Israel by heightening the sense among the contending camps that the goal of politics was to crush the other side. October 7 exposed the erosion of Israel's readiness to defend itself: the intelligence community failed to provide adequate warning, the security barrier did not impede the terrorists, and troops were elsewhere and took too long to arrive. These failures demonstrated that Israeli political unity is not some distant, discretionary goal but rather the very basis of Jewish perdurance in the Jewish people's ancient homeland.

Certainty abetted laxity and disunity. Israel's intelligence community diminished the country's security by treating as settled that Israel had no cause for concern about a major Hamas attack. Similarly, the contending political camps—Prime Minister Benjamin Netanyahu's government and the opposition—damaged the nation's civic cohesion by deeming their own political priorities as irreproachable and the other side's as irremediable.

To arrest the "virus of polarization" and restore unity, argues Goodman, Israelis must embrace "the healing power of doubt." This will involve a reorientation—moral, political, and intellectual—that derives support from the Jewish tradition, classical political philosophy, and the modern tradition of freedom. "The ability of human beings to hold opinions but not too strongly is not only a condition for a flourishing intellectual life," he writes, "but also a united and durable Israeli life." Learning to recognize the limits of one's own understanding and to appreciate the truth, doubtless partial and incomplete, in others' opinions facilitates and is facilitated by a politics of "wide agreement." Sharing the fundamental belief that Israel must remain Jewish, free, and democratic, for example, enables and is enabled by a robust exchange of opinions about law, public policy, and national security that harmonizes these sometimes-opposing principles.

Such a reorientation would reflect a discernible shift in political attitudes in Israel that has not yet translated into a political realignment. For decades, Goodman observes, the chief political battle line—indeed, the identity-defining issue—has been the Israeli-Palestinian conflict. The right sought to preserve Israeli control over the bulk of Judea and Samaria. The left aspired to make substantial territorial concessions for peace. But since the Second Intifada (2000–2005), the disagreement over the West Bank has faded: Many on the right abandoned the dream of exercising sovereignty over most of Judea and Samaria, home today to some 2.5 million to 3 million Palestinians, while many on the left lost confidence that substantial territorial compromise will bring peace.

This reconfiguration of opinions presents an opportunity for a political realignment, the crystallization of a new majority encompassing elements of the right, left, and center that recognizes that preserving Israel's hybrid character as a nation that is both a rights-protecting democracy and a Jewish state is not a luxury but a necessity. Goodman finds a nonpolitical model for this political realignment in the Israel Defense Forces and particularly in the IDF reservists who unhesitatingly responded to the call of duty on October 7 and have skillfully and bravely defended the nation since.

The IDF's combination of physical might and inner strength, maintains Goodman, exhibits Israel's hybrid character. The IDF's physical might springs from the modern tradition of freedom, which fosters entrepreneurship and innovation, whose fruits transformed Israel's military into a marvel of high-tech capabilities. IDF troops' inner strength—the disposition of right, left, and center in the regular military as well as in the reserves to put aside political grievances and risk their lives side-by-side to defend their nation—reflects traditional virtues. These are nourished by the Jewish tradition, which situates individuals within families, communities, and the nation and imposes responsibilities and duties beyond private desire and personal ambition.

Reweaving the competing yet fundamental elements of the national spirit so that in Israeli social and political life, as in the IDF, they operate to unify the nation would represent a great achievement. A rewoven unity would mark a bracing victory not only for Israelis but also for the Jewish people and for friends of freedom everywhere.

34

HOW NETANYAHU CAN CONVINCE ISRAELIS, REASSURE THE US, AND SATISFY THE SAUDIS

May 12, 2024

Early last week, almost seven months after Iran-backed Hamas jihadists perpetrated heinous war crimes in Israel—murdering, raping, mutilating, and kidnapping mostly civilians—the Israel Defense Forces seized the Philadelphi Corridor, a narrow stretch of Gaza's Rafah district on the border with Egypt. Prime Minister Benjamin Netanyahu's government believes that a ground operation in Rafah will enable Israel to accomplish its principal war aims: destroy Iran-backed Hamas's ability to rule Gaza and to wage war against the Jewish state while putting pressure on the terrorists to release some 130 remaining abductees—mostly civilians, a few Americans among them—whom Hamas holds hostage in gross violation of the international laws of war.

Entering Rafah has intensified Israel's most pressing diplomatic challenges, which involve maintaining close relations with the United States, Israel's best friend and essential partner, and upgrading relations with Saudi Arabia, the largest and richest Gulf Sunni Arab monarchy. Hamas's unlawful conversion of Gaza's cities into battlefields and its illegal use of

Palestinian noncombatants as human shields have already brought about immense loss of life and massive damage to buildings and neighborhoods as Israel has exercised its right of self-defense and pursued its legitimate war aims. Both the United States and Saudi Arabia oppose a major Israeli ground operation in Rafah for fear of additional civilian casualties and destruction of civilian infrastructure. Both the United States and Saudi Arabia, moreover, have called on Israel to support the creation of a Palestinian state, which Israel has declined to do. Reassuring the United States and satisfying the Saudis will demand from Netanyahu responsible diplomacy of a high order.

Responsible diplomacy encompasses a plan for the day after Israel attains its principal war aims. This Netanyahu has failed to provide. The best available explanation for his refusal to clarify Israel's intentions is the pressure from his hard-right flank, led by Finance Minister Bezalel Smotrich and National Security Minister Itamar Ben-Gvir. At any suggestion of Palestinian self-rule in Gaza, they threaten to bring down Netanyahu's government. Yet a suggestion may be all that Netanyahu needs to thread the diplomatic needle amid Israel's seven-front war with the Islamic Republic of Iran and its regional proxies.

War on those seven fronts—Gaza, Judea and Samaria, Lebanon, Syria, Iraq, Yemen, and Iran itself—is unlikely to end anytime soon. While the IDF has substantially degraded Hamas's ability to wage war and rule Gaza, Jerusalem cannot achieve the "absolute victory" Netanyahu has repeatedly promised. Hamas is too integrated into Gazan society and too entwined with Palestinian hearts and minds. But by maintaining ultimate security control over Gaza for the short and intermediate term, Israel can greatly reduce the threat that Hamas poses.

Gaza, though, is just one front in Iran's war on the Jewish state. Israel operates daily to counter Hamas in Judea and Samaria. In addition, Israel has caused substantial damage to Iran-backed Hezbollah in the low-intensity aerial war Hezbollah launched in southern Lebanon shortly after Hamas's October 7 attacks, but some 80,000 Israelis remain unable to return to their homes in the north because of constant drone and rocket attacks, as well as fear of a surprise ground invasion by Hezbollah's Radwan forces positioned close to the border. Notwithstanding Israel's early-April killing in Damascus of several senior commanders of Iran's Islamic Revolutionary Guard Corps, Syria remains a transit point for weapons heading from Tehran to Lebanon. Despite Israel's remarkable air-defense capabilities—on the evening of April 13, with the assistance of the United States, Britain, France, and moderate Arab nations, the Jewish state intercepted approximately 300 Iranian drones and missiles—Hezbollah maintains an arsenal of some 150,000 rockets and missiles, and Iranian proxy forces in Syria, Iraq, and Yemen possess drones and missiles capable of reaching Israel.

To meet this array of perils, Israel needs friends and partners. None is more important to Israel than the United States.

According to the Council on Foreign Relations, "Israel has long been the leading recipient of US foreign aid . . . and has privileged access to the most advanced US military platforms and technologies." Not least, America supplies the backbone of Israel's air forces—F15s, F16s, and F35s—along with the spare parts essential to the upkeep of these high-tech combat-aircraft marvels. In addition, since the October 7 attacks the United States has maintained an "extraordinary flow of aid" that "has included tank and artillery ammunition, bombs, rockets, and small arms." It is hard to see how Israel can accomplish its long-term military objectives without this equipment.[1] Consequently, the Biden administration's decision in early May to delay the delivery of some 3,500 bombs to Israel[2] and the president's statement in a May 8 CNN interview that he will withhold weapons if Israel proceeds with an attack on Hamas's

1 Jonathan Masters and Will Merrow, "US Aid to Israel in Four Charts," Council on Foreign Relations, May 24, 2024, https://www.cfr.org/article/us-aid-israel-four-charts.

2 Barak Ravid, "US Put a Hold on an Ammunition Shipment to Israel," Axios, May 5, 2024, https://www.axios.com/2024/05/05/israel-us-ammunition-shipment-hold.

stronghold in Rafah represent shots across the bow. They also send the atrocious message to Israel, other friends and partners, and not least, Hamas and other adversaries, that the jihadists' fiendish use of Palestinian civilians as human shields works.

Saudi Arabia, too, plays a key role in Israeli diplomacy. The 2020 Trump administration–brokered Abraham Accords, which normalized relations between Israel and the United Arab Emirates and Israel and Bahrain, would not have been signed had the Saudis objected. Since 2023 and with increasing openness, the Saudis have expressed interest in normalizing relations with Israel. Like the UAE and Bahrain, Saudi Arabia sees vital opportunities to cooperate with Israel in countering their common adversary Iran and expects to gain substantial benefits from commerce and trade with the Jewish state.

Saudi normalization, however, comes with a price. Crown Prince and Prime Minister Mohammed bin Salman has made clear that normalization would require the United States to sell more advanced weapons to the Saudis, cooperate in the creation of a Saudi civil nuclear program, and enter a formal defensive alliance with the kingdom. In addition, Riyadh insists, as does the United States, that Israel show progress in promoting the establishment of a Palestinian state.

The Biden administration has indicated its willingness to meet Saudi requirements. Israel has not.

Although he emphasized his determination to normalize relations with Saudi Arabia after regaining the prime ministership in November 2022, Netanyahu has little room to maneuver. In the current circumstances, his base and more than a few members of the opposition view calls for the prompt recognition of a Palestinian state as rewarding horrific terrorism. They are persuaded, moreover, that owing to the notorious corruption and weakness of the Palestinian Authority, a PA-governed state would swiftly fall into Hamas's hands and become another forward Iranian base on Israel's border. Meanwhile, elements of the hard right led by Smotrich and Ben-Gvir seem determined to renew Israeli settlements in Gaza—in 2005 Prime Minister Ariel Sharon's government withdrew all soldiers and civilians from there—among the strip's 2.3 million Palestinians.

The question for Netanyahu is how to meet Saudi Arabia's and the United States's minimum requirements concerning a Palestinian state while honoring the widespread aversion in Israel to the idea and dodging his hard-right coalition partners' threats of mutiny at the prospect.

Netanyahu's groundbreaking 2009 Bar Ilan speech provides the model. Fifteen years ago, under pressure from President Barack Obama, Netanyahu became Israel's first conservative prime minister to endorse a Palestinian state. But he stressed two crucial conditions: The Palestinians would need to recognize Israel as the nation-state of the Jewish people, and the state would have to be demilitarized.

These conditions were reasonable. They were also unacceptable, Netanyahu knew, to the Palestinians. Affirming the two-state principle while bringing into focus Palestinian opposition to Israel's reasonable requirements enabled Netanyahu to placate the Obama administration while assuaging his base and retaining his governing coalition.

The issue resurfaced in 2015. While campaigning for reelection, members of Netanyahu's Likud Party declared that "a demilitarized Palestinian state that would recognize the Jewish state" had been made irrelevant by Middle East realities. Netanyahu offered a more nuanced assessment. His office issued a statement explaining that "Prime Minister Netanyahu has made clear for years that given the current conditions in the Middle East, any territory that is given will be seized by the radical Islam just like what happened in Gaza and in southern Lebanon."[3]

That security assessment holds true today. Furthermore, Palestinian leadership is again highly unlikely to formally recognize Israel as the nation-state of the Jewish people and accept a demilitarized state.

---

3 Barak Ravid, "Netanyahu: Bar-Ilan 2-State Speech No Longer Relevant in Today's Reality," *Haaretz*, March 8, 2015, https://www.haaretz.com/2015-03-08/ty-article/.premium/bar-ilan-speech-no-longer-relevant/0000017f-ef07-d0f7-a9ff-efc790e10000.

That means that Netanyahu could thread the diplomatic needle in 2024 as he did in 2009. By reaffirming the same principles, he could reassure the United States and satisfy the Saudis. By insisting on the same reasonable conditions, he would highlight the obstacles on the Palestinian side to the principles' short-term implementation, which may convince his base and coalition partners to go along.

This will strike many as cynical and manipulative. To the contrary, affirming a long-term goal while illuminating the circumstances that prevent its near-term achievement is an essential part of responsible diplomacy. It would also open the door to near-term and intermediate-term steps that will enable Israel, once it destroys Hamas's capacity to wage war and govern and secures the hostages' release, to provide for its national security while incrementally increasing Palestinian self-rule.

35

ISRAEL'S INTEREST IN PLANNING FOR "THE DAY AFTER"

June 30, 2024

TEL AVIV—Almost nine months ago, thousands of Iran-backed Hamas jihadists stormed across Israel's southwest border to massacre, mutilate, rape, and kidnap Jews, most of whom were civilians, and take some 250 hostages, also mostly civilians. In late October Israel launched a major ground campaign in Gaza, which has substantially degraded Hamas's capacity to commit such mass depredations and to engage in military operations. Despite extraordinary efforts to target combatants, Israel Defense Forces have caused heavy casualties among noncombatant Palestinians and extensive destruction of Gaza's urban infrastructure. Hamas acquired presumptive moral and legal responsibility for that death and destruction owing to its reprehensible decision—carefully conceived, determinedly executed, and in flagrant violation of the international laws of war—to locate its headquarters, fighters, and arsenals among and beneath Gaza's civilian population.

The jihadists' depravity does not diminish Israel's responsibility under the international laws of war to minimize, to the extent possible consistent with eliminating the threat posed by Hamas, civilian casualties and damage to civilian infrastructure. Nor does Hamas's depravity, and its presumptive moral and legal responsibility for the carnage and devastation, lessen Israel's national security interest in the stabilization, reconstruction, and provision of security for postwar Gaza.

Despite the passage of nine months, Israel seems to have made only modest progress in devising an actionable plan for "the day after" the IDF accomplishes the nation's major war aims in Gaza: dismantle and destroy Hamas's military and governing capabilities and secure the release of the 116 remaining hostages. At the annual Herzliya Conference last week, Israeli National Security Advisor Tzachi Hanegbi stated that a process "for countries that want to see a governing alternative to Hamas in Gaza, with local leadership in Gaza" is "starting to take form now."

Why has the planning taken so long?

Some Israelis observe that the war's immediacy impedes the formulation of long-term strategy. Comparisons to the United States illuminate the point.

For the last 75 years, to report for duty on the front lines of America's wars—Korea, Vietnam, Afghanistan, Iraq—US soldiers have had to board an airplane or ship and journey halfway around the world. Indeed, since the Union defeated the Confederacy in the American Civil War 150 years ago, American troops have for the most part traveled overseas to reach combat zones.

For Israel, war has been largely a local affair. With light traffic, IDF soldiers setting out by car from this Mediterranean beach city can reach the southern front just across the border with Gaza in less than an hour. It takes about two hours to drive to the northern front with Iran-backed Hezbollah along Israel's border with Lebanon.

Israelis experience their multifront war with Hamas in the south and Hezbollah in the north in another way that differs dramatically from America at war. Military service in the United States is voluntary; active duty and reserve troops combined comprise less than 1 percent of the population. In contrast, Israel imposes mandatory military service on young men and women, and reserve duty continues until the age of 40 for soldiers and longer for officers. (Last week Israel's Supreme Court invalidated the exemption from mandatory military service enjoyed by ultra-Orthodox Jews; Arab citizens' exemption remains.) That means that a large percentage of non-ultra-Orthodox Jewish Israelis either serve in the IDF or have a child, sibling, spouse, or parent in uniform.

At this fraught moment, Israelis fear for the hostages, worry about frontline soldiers, mourn the victims of October 7 and the fallen soldiers, attend to the wounded, feel anxiety about the weakened economy, and expect that the low-intensity conflict with heavily armed Hezbollah will explode into a high-intensity war. So preoccupied, citizens have not demanded from the politicians and military establishment a plan for postwar Gaza.

But what about the politicians and the military establishment, not least the prime minister who leads the government? Planning for national security contingencies is a crucial element of their job descriptions.

According to the opposition's harsh criticism, planning for postwar Gaza conflicts with Prime Minister Benjamin Netanyahu's interest in prolonging the war. Keeping the nation's focus on the fighting, critics say, enables Netanyahu to delay the country's convening of a formal state investigatory commission to hold accountable those, first and foremost the prime minister, who presided over the worst security catastrophe in Israel's history. Prolonging the fighting also, they contend, provides an excuse to postpone his testimony in his corruption trial. Furthermore, argues the opposition, Netanyahu's government depends on hard-right coalition partners, Finance Minister Bezalel Smotrich and National Security Minister Itamar Ben-Gvir, who reject the very idea of a day after. Instead, they envisage Israel's civilian resettlement of, and establishment of permanent Israeli rule in, Gaza.

Meanwhile, Netanyahu's defenders say that Israel's longest-serving prime minister proceeds cautiously. He prefers to weigh options, hold his cards close to his vest, and keep the nation's adversaries, and the internal opposition, guessing. As events unfold, the prime minister's camp argues, Netanyahu modifies his views. They point out that he has offered thoughts on "the day after." In December 2023 he outlined Israel's "three requisites of peace" in the *Wall Street Journal*: "Destroy Hamas, demilitarize Gaza, and deradicalize the whole of Palestinian society." When the IDF completes its principal tasks, maintain Netanyahu loyalists, the prime minister will reveal his plans to accomplish these daunting goals.

But planning can't wait. Creating organizational structure, choosing and training personnel, raising money, drafting contracts, and more demand considerable time and effort. Whatever the complex of factors accounting for the government's refusal to articulate a full-fledged plan and stand up a team, the result is to undercut Israel's interest in stabilizing, reconstructing, and securing Gaza. That is the central argument of "Israel's War of Regime Change Is Repeating America's Mistakes," which *Foreign Affairs* published online in mid-June.

The article's three coauthors know a great deal about America's efforts to effect regime change in Iraq. David Petraeus, a partner at global investment firm KKR, served as director of the CIA, commander of the coalition forces in Iraq and Afghanistan, and commander of the US Central Command. Meghan L. O'Sullivan, director of the Belfer Center for Science and International Affairs at Harvard's Kennedy School of Government, served as special assistant to the president and deputy national security advisor for Iraq and Afghanistan. Richard Fontaine, CEO of the Center for a New American Security, worked on foreign policy in the State Department, White House, and Senate. "As the United States did in Iraq in 2003," they stress, "Israel began its war without a plan to create a governing structure, in its case to replace Hamas, and no clear blueprint has emerged after months of fighting."

The authors believe that Israel rightly resolved that Hamas must not be allowed to continue to rule Gaza. However, they warn, in the justified pursuit of regime change in Gaza, Israel is repeating "fateful strategic errors" that the United States made in Afghanistan and Iraq, "including some of the most glaring mistakes that the United States made in the early years of the Iraq war." At the same time, Petraeus, O'Sullivan, and Fontaine counsel that Israel "can also learn from some of the successes of the American campaigns—especially those of the 'surge' strategy that Washington adopted in Iraq beginning in 2007."

America's worst error in Iraq, according to the authors, was supposing that "killing and capturing terrorists" was enough. The most important lesson for Israel is that "the key to solidifying security gains and stemming the recruitment of new adversaries is holding territory, protecting civilians, and providing governance and services to them."

The authors recognize that Israel faces greater challenges in Gaza than did the United States in Iraq. Israel, for example, confronts hundreds of miles of tunnels under civilian populations. Its small standing army, which is designed for high-tech warfare and quick and decisive victories, is enmeshed in protracted urban fighting. And the Jewish state must balance the requirements of victory with the imperative to return the hostages. Nevertheless, assert the authors, "What is beyond dispute is that until some force, Israeli or otherwise, can clear Hamas fighters, hold territory, and build basic infrastructure and governing mechanisms in Gaza over the medium term, Hamas will very likely continue to reconstitute itself."

Private organizations have developed worthy proposals for postwar Gaza. MIND Israel has circulated an unpublished policy paper, "Turning Catastrophe into a Vision: MIND Israel 2024 National Strategy for a Post-Hamas Gaza (January 2024)." In addition, the Gaza Futures Task Force of the Jewish Institute for National Security of America and the Vandenburg Coalition (I serve on the advisory board) has made publicly available "The Day After: Action Plan."

But it is not enough to recognize that some combination of partners—including Arab states, the United States, other nations, and NGOs and international organizations—should assist with humanitarian relief; that Israel must work with partners to ensure security; and that Israel and partners must find local Palestinians with the fewest ties possible to Hamas to reconstitute government in Gaza. It is also urgent to appoint officials, conduct focused diplomacy, raise funds, form and prepare operational units, craft lines of effort, and accomplish an array of related tasks.

Rigorous planning for "the day after" would advance Jerusalem's vital interest in stabilizing and reconstructing Gaza, and ensuring Israel's security.

36

ISRAEL AND THE NEXT US ADMINISTRATION

July 14, 2024

According to an oft-repeated Israeli story from the 1960s, when an aide mentioned a drought, Prime Minister Levi Eshkol worriedly asked, "Where?" "In the Negev," explained the aide. "Thank God it's not in the US, then I'd be really concerned," said Eshkol.

Surrounded by what they call Iran's "ring of fire" and battling simultaneously on multiple fronts, Israelis can be excused for giving less attention these days to their country's dependence on America's wellbeing. Israeli ground forces are operating within Rafah and other densely populated urban areas in Gaza against Iran-backed Hamas. Hamas's diabolical strategy of using Palestinian civilians as human shields ensures that Israel's legitimate efforts to defend itself against the jihadists' expressed genocidal aims will cause extensive injury and death to Palestinian civilians and leave Gazan civilian infrastructure in ruins. The photos of civilian suffering have, as Hamas intended, inflicted a grievous blow on Israel's reputation, which has sunk to new lows in the court of international public opinion.

Meanwhile, Iran-backed Hezbollah's daily aerial assaults—beginning shortly after Hamas's October 7 massacre of some 1,200, mostly civilian Israelis and including Americans, and kidnapping of approximately 250 others, mostly civilian Israelis and including Americans—compelled Israel to evacuate a five-kilometer-wide swath of sovereign territory along its northern border and prepare for a high-intensity war. And Iran has equipped proxies in Syria, Iraq, and Yemen with long-range drones and missiles.

Notwithstanding Israel's focus on its soldiers, its kidnapped citizens, and its homeland, the nation's fight against Hamas, Hezbollah, other Iranian proxies, and Iran itself remains bound up with American power and prosperity. Lacking a comprehensive domestic weapons industry, Israel acquires fighter aircraft, a wide range of munitions, and other essential military equipment from the United States. Israel's fortunes at the United Nations, in the International Court of Justice and the International Criminal Court, and among nations turn in no small measure on the tone set, judgments issued, and actions taken by the United States. And should war with heavily armed Hezbollah broaden into a regional conflict—which may well include waves of Iran-launched attack drones, cruise missiles, and ballistic missiles—Washington's decision about whether and how to intervene would have major ramifications for Israel.

Hence, American politics and opinions about Israel in the United States continue to possess vital significance for the Jewish state. In the short term, the most important opinions issue from the White House and, to a lesser extent, Congress; Israel can glean these from firsthand observation and shape them through diplomatic exchange. In the long term, the American people's perceptions and judgments will prove decisive. The Jewish state's best bet for influencing these consists in serving as a strong and reliable American partner and providing an inspiring example of freedom and democracy. In the intermediate term, Israel has a keen interest in anticipating and planning for the next president's foreign policy. But who will US voters choose in November, and what understanding of America and the world will prevail?

The July/August issue of *Foreign Affairs* provides overviews of two main possibilities. Ben Rhodes, former deputy national security advisor for strategic communications during all eight years of Barack Obama's presidency, represents the Democrats. Rhodes urges the United States "to minimize enormous risks and pursue new opportunities" by adopting "an updated conception of US leadership—one tailored to a world that has moved on from American primacy and the eccentricities of American politics." Making the case for Republicans is Robert O'Brien, who served from 2019 to 2021 as national security advisor to President Donald Trump. Invoking presidents Washington, Roosevelt, Reagan, and Trump, O'Brien argues for "peace through strength." Rhodes's and O'Brien's conflicting views on Israel and the Middle East give a good sense of their slogans' practical meanings and how their parties are disposed to conduct US diplomacy.

In "A Foreign Policy for the World as It Is," Rhodes sides with many progressive critics of US foreign policy who favor "abandoning a mindset of American primacy." He joins the hard left at home and abroad in condemning not only Israel's exercise of its right to self-defense but also America's support of it. "Indeed, after Hamas's October 7 attack on Israel and the Israeli military campaign in Gaza, American rhetoric about the rules-based international order has been seen around the world on a split screen of hypocrisy, as Washington has supplied the Israeli government with weapons used to bombard Palestinian civilians with impunity," writes Rhodes. "The war has created a policy challenge for an administration that criticizes Russia for the same indiscriminate tactics that Israel has used in Gaza, a political challenge for a Democratic Party with core constituencies who don't understand why the president has supported a far-right government that ignores the United States' advice, and a moral crisis for a country whose foreign policy purports to be driven by universal values."

Rhodes swallows whole the odious canard that Israel's military operates lawlessly. He fails, however, to provide the slightest evidence that the

Jewish state could accomplish its legitimate war aims with substantially less force. At the same time, Rhodes ignores Hamas's grotesque violations of the international laws of war—slaughtering, raping, mutilating, and kidnapping civilians while hiding behind, among, and under its own civilian population—and the centrality of these reprehensible tactics to the jihadists' ambitions to eradicate Israel. Like campus protesters throughout America, Rhodes deplores US failure to thwart Israel's military operations in Gaza. "Put simply," he maintains, "Gaza should shock Washington out of the muscle memory that guides too many of its actions."

Rhodes's rebuke of US Middle East policy goes well beyond Gaza. President Trump's signal Middle East achievements, argues Rhodes, undermined peace. "By moving the US embassy in Israel from Tel Aviv to Jerusalem, recognizing the annexation of the Golan Heights, and pursuing the Abraham Accords," according to Rhodes, Trump "cut the Palestinians out of Arab-Israeli normalization and emboldened Israel's far right, lighting a fuse that detonated in the current war." Rhodes overlooks the Palestinians' resolute opposition to US-brokered peace initiatives by four presidents: Clinton, Bush, Obama, and Trump. He also fails to see that whereas Palestinian intransigence has produced an impasse, the Trump administration's bold steps, welcomed by Israel and Gulf Arabs, enhanced regional stability and provided new opportunities to ease the Israeli-Palestinian conflict. Notwithstanding Hamas's October 7 massacre and the seven-front war that Iran wages against Israel, the Abraham Accords remain in place.

In sharp contrast to Rhodes, in "The Return of Peace through Strength," O'Brien recognizes Israel as a close American friend and partner, affirms Jerusalem's legitimate war aims, and identifies the Islamic Republic of Iran as the principal threat to regional stability. Accordingly, O'Brien argues, "[T]he United States should continue to back Israel as it seeks to eliminate Hamas in Gaza." Moreover, he writes, "[T]he long-term governance and status of the territory are not for Washington to dictate;

the United States should support Israel, Egypt, and US allies in the Gulf as they grapple with that problem. But Washington should not pressure Israel to return to negotiations over a long-term solution to the broader conflict with the Palestinians." Instead, "the focus of US policy in the Middle East should remain the malevolent actor that is ultimately most responsible for the turmoil and killing: the Iranian regime."

Iran, O'Brien emphasizes, has grown stronger and more belligerent under the Biden administration. The current White House has enabled Tehran to increase oil revenues by tens of billions of dollars over the last three and a half years. During the Biden administration, Tehran "has managed to reach a point where it can not only produce nuclear weapons on-demand but produce large quantities of WGU [weapons-grade uranium] quickly in a very hard-to-destroy enrichment plant," reports the Institute for Science and International Security.[1] And the Biden administration encouraged Tehran's diplomatic rehabilitation.[2] Furthermore, observes O'Brien, "Iran's proxies, including Hamas, kidnap and kill Americans. And in April, for the first time, Iran attacked Washington's closest ally in the Middle East, Israel, directly from Iranian territory, firing hundreds of drones and missiles."

Diminishing Iran's ability to export jihadist terror "would also lead to a more productive approach to the Israeli-Palestinian conflict, which is once again roiling the region," maintains O'Brien. "For decades, the conventional wisdom held that resolving that dispute was the key to improving security in the Middle East. But the conflict has become more of a symptom than a cause of tumult in the region, the true source of which is Iran's revolutionary, theocratic regime." Tehran "provides critical

---

1 David Albright, "Technical Note: Iran's Recent Increase in Enrichment Capacity at the Fordow Enrichment Plant," Institute for Science and International Security, June 19, 2024, https://isis-online.org/isis-reports/mobile/technical-note-irans-recent-increase-in-enrichment-capacity-at-fordow.

2 Patsy Widakuswara, "White House Welcomes Chinese-Brokered Saudi-Iran Deal," *Voice of America*, March 10, 2023, https://www.voanews.com/a/white-house-welcomes-chinese-brokered-saudi-iran-deal/6999700.html.

funding, arms, intelligence, and strategic guidance to an array of groups that threaten Israel's security."

Although preoccupied with the grind of daily battle with barbarous jihadists, Israelis have cause to follow carefully events transpiring in the United States and to prepare for their far-reaching repercussions. Whether the next American president renounces US primacy in world affairs or returns to the pursuit of peace through strength is a choice that will have weighty consequences for the Jewish state and for America's interests in Middle East stability and global order.

37

EXPLAINING ISRAEL'S JUST WAR OF SELF-DEFENSE TO AMERICA

August 4, 2024

On July 27 Iran-backed Hezbollah launched a rocket from southern Lebanon—part of the militia's near-constant bombardment of northern Israel since October 8, 2023—striking a soccer field on the Golan Heights and killing 12 Israeli Druze children and wounding dozens more. Israeli Prime Minister Benjamin Netanyahu promised a "harsh" response. Thus far, in Beirut, Israel has killed Hezbollah's most senior military commander while in Tehran, exiled Iran-backed Hamas political chief Ismail Haniyeh was killed, according to the *New York Times*, by a bomb smuggled into the state guesthouse where he stayed. Both Hezbollah and Iran have vowed to exact revenge. Diplomats fear a ruinous regional war. In part to explain the larger historical and geopolitical context of Israel's multifront war with the Islamic Republic of Iran and its proxies, Netanyahu addressed a joint session of Congress on July 24 at the invitation of House Speaker Mike Johnson.

That day thousands of anti-Israel protesters, many wearing kaffiyehs, took to the streets of Washington to denounce Netanyahu and Israel.

Cries of "Free, free Palestine" rang out on Capitol Hill. Signs screamed "Arrest Netanyahu" and "End all US aid to Israel." Rioters defaced American monuments with pro-Hamas graffiti and took down and burned American flags.

Although the rioters regard Israel and America as criminally culpable for the Gaza carnage and Hamas as blameless, the gruesome facts say otherwise. On October 7, 2023, Hamas jihadists invaded southern Israel, massacring some 1,200 people, among them several Americans, and kidnapping around 250, including several Americans. Over the last 10 months, Israel has sought to secure the hostages' return while destroying Hamas's ability to wage war and govern Gaza. Israeli military operations, according to Hamas's Gaza Health Ministry, have killed almost 40,000 Palestinians, though that number does not distinguish between combatants and noncombatants. Fighting has reduced large swaths of Gaza to rubble. Yet Hamas can end the fighting instantly by laying down its arms, releasing the remaining hostages, and renouncing its formal commitment to destroy the Jewish state.

Netanyahu's powerful if problematic speech before Congress countered the intense anti-Israel propaganda that has distorted American views. While major Israeli political figures praised the remarks, Netanyahu's visit provoked consternation, even outrage, among Israel's domestic opposition. They deplored Congress's invitation to Netanyahu and President Biden's White House meeting with him.

Thirty-three distinguished Israelis—from national security, government, commerce, and the academy—published an open letter to congressional leaders arguing that Netanyahu should be seen as beyond the pale. He remains on trial for bribery, fraud, and breach of trust. He was recently served notice by an Israeli state commission of inquiry, which is looking into Israel's and Egypt's purchases of submarines from a German company, that he is suspected of making "decisions that endangered national security and harmed Israel's foreign relations." And critics maintain he tore the country apart last year with an ill-conceived proposal to overhaul the judiciary, shoulders responsibility for the worst security lapse in Israel's history, and after more than nine months of fighting has not defeated Hamas, freed the hostages, advanced a plausible plan for stabilizing and governing postwar Gaza, or established quiet on the northern border.

These Israeli opposition grievances played into American progressives' long-standing antipathy toward Netanyahu, whom they see as the chief obstacle to establishing a Palestinian state. About half of House and Senate Democrats—as well as Vice President Harris, who would normally preside over a joint session of Congress—skipped the prime minister's speech.

Nevertheless, in plain but rousing language, Netanyahu made a compelling case for America to support wholeheartedly Israel's fight against the "ring of fire" that Iran has built around the Jewish state. Iran-funded militias—Hamas in Gaza, Hamas in Judea and Samaria, Hezbollah in Lebanon, Houthis in Yemen, proxies in Syria and Iraq—and Tehran itself seek not only Israel's destruction but also the defeat and subjugation of the American-led West. "Our enemies are your enemies, our fight is your fight, and our victory will be your victory," Netanyahu declared. "Working together, I'm confident that our two nations will vanquish the tyrants and terrorists who threaten us both."

Netanyahu stressed the failure of pro-Hamas protesters "to make the simple distinction between those who target terrorists and those who target civilians, between the democratic State of Israel and the terrorist thugs of Hamas." That elementary distinction conflicts with the interests of a key patron of the protesters. "We recently learned from the US director of national intelligence," said Netanyahu, "that Iran is funding and promoting anti-Israel protests in America."

Netanyahu also rebutted the protesters' blood libel that Israel is committing genocide against Gazans by starving and targeting them. "Israel has enabled more than 40,000 aid trucks to enter Gaza," he stated. "That's half a million tons of food, and that's more than 3,000 calories [per day] for every man, woman and child in Gaza. If there are Palestinians in Gaza who aren't getting enough food, it's not because Israel is blocking it, it's because Hamas is stealing it."

The charge that Israel deliberately targets civilians is just as false and obscene. "The IDF has dropped millions of flyers, sent millions of text messages, made hundreds of thousands of phone calls to get Palestinian civilians out of harm's way," said Netanyahu. "But at the same time, Hamas does everything in its power to put Palestinian civilians in harm's way. They fire rockets from schools, from hospitals, from mosques." They take pride in those "Palestinian women and children" who "excel at being human shields." And they "shoot their own people when they try to leave the war zone."

One reason that Netanyahu devoted a significant portion of his speech to setting the record straight about both Israel's extraordinary steps to honor the international laws of war and Hamas's boundless defiance of them is the Biden administration's dereliction of duty. It has done too little to clarify to Americans Israel's just-war aims and the US national interest in Israel's defeat of the jihadists and could do much more to parry anti-Israel propaganda.

Nevertheless, and quite properly, Netanyahu expressed gratitude to President Biden "for half a century of friendship to Israel and for being, as he says, a proud Zionist," as well as "for his heartful support for Israel after the savage attack on October 7." Biden's support has been rhetorical, material, and highly personal. "He rightly called Hamas 'sheer evil,'" recalled Netanyahu. "He dispatched two aircraft carriers to the Middle East to deter a wider war. And he came to Israel to stand with us during our darkest hour, a visit that will never be forgotten."

Nor is that all that President Biden and his administration have done to advance Israeli war efforts. Notwithstanding controversy over the provision of heavy bombs in connection to Israel's Rafah operation, the administration has overseen the delivery of billions of dollars of vital munitions and additional military equipment to the Israel Defense Forces.

In mid-April, the United States led a coalition that operated with the IDF to fend off the more than 300 drones, cruise missiles, and ballistic missiles launched by Iran at the Jewish state. The administration has on many occasions reaffirmed Israel's right to defend itself and condemned antisemitism. In May, Biden called the International Criminal Court application for arrest warrants of top Israelis "outrageous" and rejected any equivalence between Israel's actions to defeat Hamas and Hamas terrorism.

At the same time, the Biden administration has lent credence to the anti-Israel protesters through its skewed framing of the issues.

The administration placed the onus on Israel to agree to a ceasefire and treated Americans killed and kidnapped by Hamas as a peripheral issue. The White House should have demanded immediately and often that Hamas unconditionally surrender and release all the hostages.

The administration implied, or let stand the accusation, that Israel bears primary responsibility for the suffering of Gaza Palestinians. The White House should have consistently and forcefully blamed Hamas for the humanitarian disaster unfolding in Gaza. Hamas's October 7 massacre, its kidnapping of civilians, and its military operations in and under Gaza's cities manifestly violate the international laws of war. This grotesque illegality is the source of the humanitarian disaster in Gaza, which Hamas could end at any moment by ceasing to fight, freeing the hostages, and repudiating its ambitions to destroy Israel.

And the administration declined to tell the American people that Gaza was one of seven fronts in Iran's war against Israel. The White House should have explained that this multifront war against the Jewish state does not end with Israel. It is also directed at America's Gulf Arab partners and ultimately at the United States, liberal democracies, and their principles of individual freedom and human equality.

As Israel enters the eleventh month of its war of self-defense against Iran and its proxies, the administration owes it to the American people to explain America's interest in, and the justice of, Israeli victory.

38

THE WIDER MIDDLE EAST WAR THAT ONLY HAMAS WANTS

August 9, 2024, discussing "Israel's Next War" by Amos Harel

The Middle East teeters on the brink of a ruinous all-out regional war. Yet Israel did not want a wider and high-intensity war. Iran-backed Hezbollah does not appear to have wanted a wider and high-intensity war. And Iran, too, appears not to have wanted a wider and high-intensity war. Only Iran-backed Hamas wanted a full-blown regional war. It may well get its way.

In defending itself against Iran's "ring of fire"—Hamas in Gaza and the West Bank, Hezbollah in Lebanon, Houthis in Yemen, militias in Syria and Iraq, and Tehran itself—intended to wear it down and cause its collapse, Israel advances American interests in regional stability and in fortifying an international order that favors freedom and democracy. American support for Israel, in the military arena as well as in the court of international public opinion, has been and will remain crucial.

Committed by its charter to Israel's destruction, Hamas launched a savage attack on southern Israel on October 7, 2023, targeting mostly civilians and killing more than 1,200, around 40 of whom were Americans, and kidnapping more than 250, around 10 of whom were Americans. Igniting a multifront war belonged to "the contours of Hamas's broader plan," according to a November 2023 *Washington Post* assessment. Hamas's aim was "not just to kill and capture Israelis, but to spark a conflagration that would sweep the region and lead to a wider conflict." In a meeting convened by the *New York Times* with Hamas representatives in Qatar that also took place in November, Taher El-Nounou, a Hamas media advisor, said, "I hope that the state of war with Israel will become permanent on all the borders, and that the Arab world will stand with us."

Yahya Sinwar—leader of Hamas in Gaza and recently named head of the overall organization's Political Bureau to replace Ismail Haniyeh, who was killed in Tehran last week—recognized that Gaza Palestinians would pay a high price for Hamas's success. In June 2024 the *Wall Street Journal* reported that the mastermind of the October 7 attacks affirmed in emails to Hamas negotiators that the thousands of civilian deaths in Gaza involved "necessary sacrifices" for the sake of Israel's annihilation.

Writing to Hamas officials negotiating a ceasefire agreement, Sinwar boasted, "We have the Israelis right where we want them"—bogged down fighting Hamas militants dressed as civilians in and under Gaza's cities.

As Sinwar anticipated, the international media cooperated with his plan by portraying Israel as responsible for the humanitarian disaster in Gaza. Yet Palestinian civilian suffering in Gaza on a mass scale was, for Sinwar, a foreseeable and intended consequence of Hamas's slaughter of Israeli civilians on October 7 and of the jihadists' determination, decades in the making, to unlawfully and inhumanely embed Hamas military forces in Gaza's civilian areas, including homes, schools, hospitals, and mosques. Sinwar may not have anticipated the resourcefulness, tenacity, and valor with which Israel would exercise its right to destroy Hamas's capacity to wage war and govern, and to secure the hostages' release. But the Hamas leader anticipated correctly the alacrity with which diplomats and international organizations would leap to blame Israel for the suffering of Gaza's Palestinian population.

Over the last month, Israel has inflicted several major blows on Iran's "ring of fire." On July 13 the Israel Defense Forces killed Hamas military chief Mohammed Deif, who had been hiding in Khan Younis in a compound located in a designated humanitarian zone. On July 20, following months of Iran-backed Houthi efforts to strike Israel from Yemen and in direct response to a Houthi drone that hit a Tel Aviv building, killing a man, IDF aircraft flew more than a thousand miles to destroy fuel-storage facilities at the Houthi-controlled Hodeida port in western Yemen. On July 30, in retaliation for the Hezbollah rocket that killed 12 children playing soccer in the Golan Heights and wounded dozens more, an IDF airstrike killed top Hezbollah military commander Fuad Shukr in an apartment building in southern Beirut. And on July 31 Hamas political leader Ismail Haniyeh was killed at a state-run guesthouse in Tehran—on one account by a remotely activated bomb and on another by a short-range projectile. Although widely believed to have executed the mission, Israel has not claimed responsibility for Haniyeh's death.

Marvels of intelligence gathering and analysis, patient planning, and pinpoint execution, such acts of self-defense against enemies devoted to its destruction come at a high cost to Israel. In particular the killing of Hezbollah's Shukr in Beirut and of Hamas's Haniyeh in Tehran humiliated their hosts and made likely retaliatory strikes from Hezbollah and Iran that could plunge the region into a full-blown war.

In "Israel's Next War," which appeared in late July online at *Foreign Affairs*, Amos Harel explains the foremost danger. The defense analyst for the Israeli newspaper *Haaretz*, Harel focuses on Hezbollah, which represents a substantially more formidable foe than Hamas and a closer and more menacing threat than Iran.

"Although Israeli air defense systems have been extremely successful thus far against missile attacks from Gaza, Lebanon, Iran, and Yemen, a total war with Hezbollah would be a whole different ballgame," Harel writes. "According to Israeli intelligence estimates, Hezbollah's weapons stockpile is more than seven times as large as Hamas's and includes far more lethal weapons." The arsenal contains "hundreds of attack drones, it includes some 130,000–150,000 rockets and missiles, including hundreds of ballistic missiles that could reach targets in Tel Aviv and even farther south—indeed, every point in the country."

Despite the many and varied wars its neighbors have compelled it to fight since its birth in 1948, Israel has never faced a remotely similar threat. "Israel's home-front command estimates that if a full-scale conflict broke out now, Hezbollah would launch some 3,000 rockets and missiles every day of the war, threatening to overwhelm Israel's missile defenses," according to Harel. "Israel would have to concentrate on defending crucial infrastructure and military bases, tell the civilian population to stay in bomb shelters, and hope for the best."

Had Hezbollah not been taken by surprise on October 7, and had it not hesitated, its fighters could well have overrun northern Israel while the nation was still reeling from Hamas's rampage through southern border communities. However, the IDF quickly moved tens of thousands of soldiers to the northern front, which stymied a Hezbollah ground assault.

At the same time, daily Hezbollah drone and rocket attacks since October 8 and the lingering peril of cross-border incursions compelled Israel to evacuate tens of thousands of civilians from a three- to five-mile swath of territory on the nation's border with Lebanon. More than 10 months later, those civilians remain displaced persons within their own country while Hezbollah's persistent aerial assaults on the north have inflicted severe damage on Israeli civilian infrastructure and ignited numerous forest fires.

While caught off guard by Hamas on October 7, "Israel has long been preparing for a war with Hezbollah," Harel reports. Nevertheless, Israeli Prime Minister Benjamin Netanyahu rejected a plan swiftly put forward by military leaders for "a major operation against Hezbollah that apparently would include the assassination of senior Hezbollah leaders."

Netanyahu had good reasons for exercising restraint. The Biden administration was opposed. Also, Harel argues, Netanyahu "doubted whether the army was up to the task of fighting vicious wars on multiple fronts, just days after Hamas's massacre of Israelis."

But Israel did take action against the jihadists in Lebanon. Since October 8, the IDF has, in addition to the recent elimination of Shukr, killed a senior Hamas leader in Beirut, several senior Hezbollah commanders, and at least 370 Hezbollah fighters. It has also regularly destroyed weapons convoys and depots, and rocket launchers.

At the moment, US Special Envoy Amos Hochstein has little prospect of securing a negotiated settlement. Israel insists, in accordance with the August 2006 ceasefire agreement formalized in UN Security Council Resolution 1701, that Hezbollah forces remain north of the Litani River in southern Lebanon, about seven to 20 miles from the border as the waterway wends from east to west. Hezbollah wants to return to the illegal positions it occupied before October 7 south of the Litani and close to the border.

Consequently, the Israeli military establishment generally believes that a showdown with Hezbollah is inevitable. Israel's preparations must consider the circumstances and the timing. Two major factors are the strains on IDF troops from 10 months of fighting Hamas and Hezbollah and the shortages of equipment, including key munitions. In the event of a major war, the IDF would probably rely on intensive airstrikes along with a ground incursion to the Litani. The airstrikes "could bring massive destruction to all state-owned civilian infrastructure in Lebanon within a few days," states Harel.

At the same time, Hezbollah, perhaps also Iran and the Houthis, will rain down unprecedented waves of rockets and missiles on Israeli cities. Since Hezbollah, in blatant disregard of the international laws of war, places arsenals and launchers among civilian populations, Israeli operations to destroy those legitimate military targets will likely, though not intentionally, cause the deaths of thousands of Lebanese. Harel warns that Israel will be portrayed by "many Western countries and in the international media" not as fighting in self-defense like Ukraine but "as another Russia, almost a pariah state."

In the event of the full-blown regional war that Hamas sought to ignite on October 7, Israel's effective exercise of its right of self-defense would depend in part on US intelligence sharing, supplies, and antimissile operations. The Biden administration will also need to explain to a generally hostile and poorly informed world, not least many Western countries and the international media, that Israel's determined exercise of its right to self-defense advances America's interest in a stable Middle East that favors freedom and democracy.

39

BERNARD-HENRI LÉVY COUNTERS THE DEMONIZATION OF ISRAEL

September 8, 2024, discussing Israel Alone *by Bernard-Henri Lévy*

A mark of Israel's demonization is the contrivance of one body of international laws of war for the Jewish state alongside a separate and well-established body of laws governing armed conflict for the rest of the world. With Iran-backed Hamas's barbaric assault on Israeli civilians on October 7, 2023, and the defensive war Israel launched to destroy Hamas and rescue the hostages, that malicious double standard has reached a new peak.

In a *Mosaic* magazine essay headlined "A Special Dictionary for Israel" in January, Shany Mor, a lecturer in political thought at Reichman University in Herzliya, specified "two rhetorical functions" served by weaponizing international law against Israel. It enables critics to abjure partisan bias, claiming that universal principles compel them to condemn the Jewish state. And by casting Israel as an egregious violator of international law, international courts, diplomats, journalists, and law professors join with pro-Hamas student activists to encourage odious comparisons between Israel and the Nazis who targeted Jews for extermination.

To delegitimize the Jewish state, Israel's accusers have corruptly reconfigured key international laws-of-war concepts.

For the rest of the world, "proportionality" requires that force be proportional to the accomplishment of a legitimate military goal, which allows for foreseeable but unintended collateral damage. In Israel's case, proportionality entails that the Jewish state's military operations must not cause more harm than Israel has incurred.

For the rest of the world, "collective punishment" involves direct imposition of costs on groups not involved in the fight. In Israel's case, collective punishment encompasses the unintended and indirect effects on noncombatants of lawful military operations.

For the rest of the world, "occupation" refers to a nation's controlling presence in another state's territory. In Israel's case, occupation defines its pre-October 7 relation to Gaza even though Israel withdrew all its soldiers and civilians in 2005; Egypt controlled its side of the border with Gaza while Israel controlled its side; and Israel maintained a lawful naval blockade of Gaza to thwart the jihadists' acquisition of supplies for attacks on Israeli civilians.

And for the rest of the world, "genocide" names the deliberate destruction of a people, in part or in whole. In Israel's case, genocide describes Palestinian hardships or casualty counts deriving from Hamas's war against the Jewish state that Israel's vilifiers deem disproportional.

Bernard-Henri Lévy shows that the demonization of Israel goes well beyond the nefarious fabrication of a separate body of international law to defame and convict the Jewish state. Known internationally as BHL, he dedicates his slim new volume *Israel Alone*, as he dedicated the original French book released in March, to the 131 hostages then held by Hamas. Today fewer than 100 abductees, living and dead, remain in Gaza.

Lévy's book is many things. It is a cry from the heart from one who for decades has defended Israel against the vicious attacks to which it has been regularly subject. It is a philosophical reflection on history, memory, fidelity, and justice. And it is a summons to appreciate Israel's spectacular achievements, grasp its peril, and recognize that the nation's fight to exercise sovereignty as a rights-protecting democracy in the Jewish people's ancestral homeland has become inseparable from the defense of free and democratic nation-states against the mounting authoritarian threat.

A prominent French public intellectual—political commentator, novelist, filmmaker, and playwright—Lévy, now in his midseventies, is the author of over 40 books, has made eight films, and publishes frequently as a columnist. Trained in philosophy, he emerged in the 1970s as a leader of the "new philosophers," a young generation of French anti-Marxist intellectuals who rediscovered the virtues of the modern tradition of freedom. His writings, which glide from philosophy to history, politics, literature, and religion, have a propensity for the florid and the grandiose.

Dashing, flamboyant, wealthy, and globe-trotting, he has journeyed to war zones for 50 years to chronicle outrages against human rights. On October 8, 2023, he landed in the war zone into which Hamas had transformed Israel—to commiserate with friends, report on the atrocities, and explore the massacre's significance for Israel and the free world.

According to Lévy, "the pogrom of October 7, 2023" was not a mere event but rather, in German philosopher Reiner Schürmann's sense of the term, an "Event," possessing "historical, epochal, era-opening power." Like al-Qaeda's September 11, 2001, attacks, the October 7 slaughter was "unprecedented in form." Notwithstanding the military intelligence that should have anticipated an attack of some sort, October 7 was "unpredictable" and appears "unthinkable, incalculable." Such an Event "breaks history in two." The jihadists' savagery makes it impossible, maintains Lévy, to return to the comforting belief that history is progressive and reasonable.

The Event precipitated three "upheavals." The first involved "the alignment, for the worse, of Israel with the diaspora." Using GoPro body cameras and social networks, the jihadists broadcast around the globe a bone-chilling message: "There is nowhere in the world where Jews are safe." The second upheaval—sparked not only by the jihadists' killing, raping, mutilating, and kidnapping of Jews but also by the delight the terrorists took in the murder and mayhem—was the eruption into the civilized world of "radical evil," that is, "the evil of man devouring man." The third upheaval consisted in the rallying of anti-Western forces—"Russia, China, the Iran of the ayatollahs, neo-Ottoman Turkey, and the Arab countries prone to jihadism"—to Hamas's cause.

Widespread efforts throughout the West to erase the October 7 slaughter, argues Lévy, constituted a second Event. New York Congressman Jamaal Bowman and various "pro-Palestinian" activists, as well as an advisor to British foreign secretary David Cameron, voiced doubts that Israeli women had been raped, notwithstanding the ghastly evidence of Hamas's sexual brutalization of female soldiers and civilians.[1] Politicians, professors, and students on both sides of the Atlantic justified the killing and kidnapping of Israelis, soldiers and civilians, as the legitimate exercise of Hamas's right to resist. The Red Cross ignored or downplayed the Hamas-held captives. And UN Secretary-General António Guterres blamed October 7 on Israel's supposed occupation of Gaza. These are the tip of the iceberg.

More broadly, and already in the early months of the war, Israel's demonizers enlisted three stock arguments. They employed "the indestructible, inextinguishable, eternal 'Yes, but' so dear to professional excusers of evil." They insisted on Israel's obligation to accept a ceasefire as the Jewish state defended itself against Hamas's nightmarish aggression and battled Hezbollah in Lebanon and other Iranian regional proxies that also aimed to wipe Israel out of existence. And amid the trauma and complex war effort, they demanded that Israel collaborate in the prompt establishment of a Palestinian state, which disregarded Israel's security

1 Jeffrey Gettleman et al., "'Screams without Words': How Hamas Weaponized Sexual Violence on Oct. 7," *New York Times*, December 28, 2023, https://www.nytimes.com/2023/12/28/world/middleeast/oct-7-attacks-hamas-israel-sexual-violence.html.

and could only be seen by Jerusalem's enemies as confirming that sufficient brutality induces capitulation to their demands.

The October 7 slaughter let loose "a gale of antisemitism," not least in France and, most shockingly to Lévy, in the United States. The worst moment, he maintains, came when the Harvard, MIT, and University of Pennsylvania presidents equivocated at a congressional hearing as to whether calling for the genocide of the Jews on their campuses qualifies as harassment.

"When you realize that these three universities appear at the bottom of the free speech rankings compiled each year by the nonpartisan Foundation for Individual Rights and Expression, it is hard to avoid the following conclusion: All minorities on campus are protected against offensive comments; safe spaces and comfort zones are provided so students aren't inconvenienced by free but hurtful statements," writes Lévy. "That is, all minorities but one."

Lévy responds directly to several oft-heard accusations intended to establish Israel's guilt for the atrocities Hamas perpetrated against Israelis and for the tragic loss of Palestinian lives in Gaza.

First, rather than assimilate among the nations, Jews opted to exercise national sovereignty, he explains in the spirit of the early political Zionists, because antisemitism made a state necessary.

Second, Israel is not a "colonial" state—the smug conceit on college campuses these days—because Jewish presence in the land extends back more than 3,000 years, almost two millennia before the birth of Islam and the arrival of Arabs. Moreover, whereas in the twentieth and twenty-first centuries the Jews consistently embraced compromise over the land, the Arabs consistently rejected it.

Third, the Arab-Muslim world bears partial responsibility for the flight of Jews to Israel because of Arab-Muslim support of Nazism in World War II.

And fourth, while "civilian deaths in Gaza, including the death of children" are unintended and terrible consequences of Israel's exercise of its right to self-defense, "the responsibility for these children's deaths lies first and foremost not with Israel but with those who turned them into human shields."

A secular Jew and no stranger to Israel's shortcomings, Lévy sees in the nation's brave soldiers, in citizens' unflagging determination to bring home the hostages, and in the country's gloriously diverse Jewish and non-Jewish population stirring evidence of Israel's having kept faith with its founding principles. Countering, as he does, the rampant demonization of Israel—the free and democratic nation-state of the Jewish people—is not only admirable and just. It is also crucial to the defense of freedom and democracy in a world increasingly hostile to America's founding principles.

40

ATHENS, SPARTA, AND ISRAEL

October 6, 2024, discussing An Existential War: From Tragedy to Victory and Beyond *by Ari Shavit*

Athens and Sparta represent for classical thinkers distinct and opposing regimes. Democratic Athens took pride in its freedom, openness, and accomplishments in the arts and philosophy. Oligarchic Sparta was famous for its social stratification, strict military discipline, and battlefield prowess. The two ancient Greek cities were thought, not least by one another, to stand for rival and incompatible forms of life.

Therefore, the central assertion of Ari Shavit's slender and singular book, *An Existential War: From Tragedy to Victory and Beyond*, unsettles. To survive in a post–October 7 world in which the Islamic Republic of Iran wages a seven-front war against it, contends Shavit, Israel must combine the virtues of Athens and Sparta.

Then again, Shavit's insistence that Jerusalem must cultivate the best of Athens and Sparta is also fitting. Survival has always required Israel, amid the current "existential peril" as much as ever, to exercise simultaneously the refined virtues and the martial virtues.

The uncommon mix of the free and democratic ethic and the warrior ethic has animated Israel from the beginning. Thanks in no small part to uncommon acumen and astounding determination, Jews living in their ancestral homeland under the British mandate of Palestine in the first half of the twentieth century gave birth in May 1948—as British rule expired and five Arab nations attacked—to Israel as the nation-state of the Jewish people and as a rights-protecting democracy. Owing in significant measure to their ingenuity and fortitude, Israelis over the last 76 years have defeated and deterred numerous Arab armies and held off a variety of terrorist organizations and nonstate Islamist militias while creating a multiethnic and multireligious society, a vibrant culture, and a prosperous high-tech economy.

Drawing on wellsprings of resourcefulness and courage, shocked and heartbroken Israelis came together after the October 7 atrocities perpetrated one year ago by Iran-backed Hamas jihadists to fight the bloodthirsty enemy, comfort the bereaved, and provide essential social services. Since then, improvisation and well-conceived and skillfully executed battle plans enabled Israel to greatly diminish through treacherous urban warfare Hamas's ability to govern Gaza and wage war as the Jewish state also strives to free the hostages. With ingenuity and discipline, Israel has since late July killed Hamas political leader Ismail Haniyeh in Tehran, incapacitated thousands of Iran-backed Hezbollah fighters by detonating their communications devices, destroyed Hezbollah's Beirut headquarters and killed Hezbollah Secretary-General Hassan Nasrallah and many of his top commanders, substantially degraded the militia's stocks of rockets and missiles, and blown up Houthi military targets in Yemen.

A prominent Israeli journalist and author of the 2015 *New York Times* bestseller *My Promised Land: The Triumph and Tragedy of Israel*, Shavit excels at bringing into focus the nation's blend of virtues as well as its flaws and vulnerabilities. This broad perspective enabled him to identify early the looming peril.

From the end of the Second Intifada in the mid-2000s to the social and political crisis triggered by the judicial overhaul proposed by Prime Minister Benjamin Netanyahu's government in January 2023, Israel enjoyed years of plenty—a robust, start-up-driven economy and relative quiet. Amid the good times, Shavit warned that citizens were growing complacent even as the nation's political cohesion eroded, and Iran developed nuclear weapons and tightened its ring of jihadist militias surrounding the Jewish state.

In *Saving Israel*, a short book published in Hebrew in the spring of 2023, Shavit counseled that the "deep crisis" over Netanyahu's judicial overhaul "endangers the Israeli miracle" and "threatens to erase our sensational achievements and leave us homeless." He called on Israel's Zionist majority, embracing wide swaths of the left and the right, to form a new "Zionist covenant" reflecting a spirit at once "powerful and moral, nationalist and liberal, Jewish and democratic." Preserving that covenant demands both Spartan and Athenian virtues: "Only the combination of toughness and openness will ensure that neither weakness nor zealotry will bring us to the edge of the abyss."

With *An Existential War*—an English translation is underway—Shavit carries into the domain of grand strategy the ambition to explain the harsh realities, internal as well as external, that Israel confronts and to clarify the balance of clashing strengths that the Jewish state must summon. An array of distinguished individuals has attested to Shavit's contribution to fashioning a new national security strategy for the Jewish state. They include Israeli President Isaac Herzog, who hails from the left; former Prime Minister Naftali Bennett, who belongs to the religious right; former Israel Defense Forces Chief of Staff and Defense Minister Benny Gantz (under Netanyahu); former IDF Chief of Staff Gadi Eisenkot (also under Netanyahu); and several distinguished retired generals. All agree: With few words, Shavit goes a long way to sketching the assumptions, principles, facts, interests, threats, strategic objectives, and tactics that, in a post–October 7 world, must inform Israel's defense of its territory, people, and way of life.

Shavit begins with brute reality: Israel dwells amid daunting dangers. From its founding, the Jewish state has been "mired in a bitter, profound conflict with the powerful forces of radical Islam, Arab nationalism, and Palestinian nationalism that seek to destroy it." This makes Israel unique among the world's rights-protecting democracies: "It is a **frontier democracy**, a free society living by its sword, an advanced nation whose adversaries aspire to tear it down" (emphasis here and throughout is in the original). Sovereign Israel's almost 10 million people and 13,200 square miles of territory in the region are dwarfed by 430 million Arabs spread across 8.64 million square miles, Iran with a population of 91.5 million and a territory of 636,000 square miles, and 1.9 billion Muslims worldwide.

Israel's founding fathers developed a military doctrine that enabled the nation to not merely survive but thrive while surrounded by adversaries who could be deterred but never fully defeated. Right-wing Zionist Ze'ev Jabotinsky espoused the construction of an "iron wall" drawing on Zionism's "scientific-technological excellence, economic prowess, military supremacy, and moral-ideological fortitude." Behind it, the Jewish state could build a flourishing society grounded in the rule of law and equal rights.

For operations beyond the iron wall, left-wing Zionist David Ben-Gurion, the fledgling nation's first prime minister, devised a strategy that rested on three pillars, according to Shavit. Superior intelligence would allow Israel to mobilize quickly. Decisive victories would stop enemy armies before they could inflict damage on the Israeli homeland. And strategic deterrence would emerge from a string of major triumphs that would dishearten the enemy and reconcile it to Israel's existence.

The success of Israel's founding security doctrine brought about its obsolescence. Israel achieved stunning victories in the 1948–1949 War of Independence and the 1967 Six-Day War, and heroically turned the tide against Egypt and Syria in the 1973 Yom Kippur War. It signed peace treaties with Egypt in 1979 and Jordan in 1994. The 1993 Oslo Accords spurred hopes of ending the Israeli-Palestinian conflict. But following Oslo's demise and the exhaustion of the Second Intifada (2000–2005), Israelis lulled themselves into believing that the conflict could be managed indefinitely. Meanwhile, the military and the political echelon adopted the comforting delusion that Iranian proxies—particularly Hamas in Gaza and Hezbollah in Lebanon but also Hamas in Judea and Samaria, militias in Syria and Iraq, and the Houthis in Yemen—could be kept at bay by an IDF that was small, mobile, and high-tech.

Having served as prime minister from 1996 to 1999, Netanyahu returned to the prime ministership in 2009 and from there has led the country for 14 of the last 16 years. During this decade and a half, more and more talented Israelis opted for the private sector over politics and public service. And with affluence, to which Netanyahu's free-market policies during his 2003–2005 tenure as finance minister made a major contribution, Israelis increasingly indulged the spirit of tribalism. Identity—as Ashkenazi or Sephardi, religious or secular, anti-Netanyahu or pro-Netanyahu, member of the people or the elite—superseded the solidarity stemming from common Israeli citizenship.

During the Netanyahu years, a complacent Israel, argues Shavit, "failed to adopt a comprehensive national strategy to grapple with the dangerous geopolitical developments engulfing the Middle East and beyond." Iran and its proxies surrounded the Jewish state to the south, north, and east with sophisticated drones, rockets, and missiles. The Tehran-led jihadists aimed to steadily weaken and dispirit Israel until Iran acquired nuclear weapons and fundamentally altered the rules of the game.

Hamas, which has exercised "total control" over Gaza for almost 20 years, and Hezbollah, which has maintained "almost total control" over Lebanon for at least as long, have presented the most immediate threats. Yet Israel failed to fashion an effective military or diplomatic response to either.

Israel's state-of-the-art rocket and missile defense systems provided unprecedented protection from the terrorists' projectiles. This great technological achievement, however, compounded Israeli complacency. At the same time and with Iranian aid, Hamas and Hezbollah steadily increased the quantity and quality of their weapons, extended their tunnel systems, embedded themselves further within their own civilian populations, and refined plans and trained for murderous surprise assaults on Israeli civilians.

Israel adopted a defensive posture. "**The new, if unarticulated, objective of Israeli policy in the last decades became the protection of a state dedicated to the good life by means of minimizing casualties and lengthening the intervals between outbreaks of hostility**," writes Shavit. "The historical security doctrine was replaced by a reckless *modus operandi*." The hard truth is that "[i]n contrast to the Ben Gurion government, the Netanyahu government governed without a national strategy or a national security doctrine."

A worthy Israeli national strategy, Shavit stresses, must forthrightly address Israel's "existential challenge," which consists of three threats. The first is Iran: "[F]or the first time in its history, Israel **confronts a regional power with strategic capabilities, a strategic masterplan, an imperial past, and imperial ambitions**." The second is terrorism: The jihadists are a "fanatical adversary" conducting "**a long-term asymmetric campaign**" against a prosperous and law-abiding nation-state. By hiding and fighting from within and under its own civilian populations, the terrorists expose Israel to international obloquy because of the necessary measures it must take to defend itself. And by attacking Israel's civilian population, the terrorists hope to exhaust and dispirit the Jewish state. The third is the combined threat: Together Iran and its jihadist proxies "strive to combine **eleventh-century values with twenty-first-century capabilities**."

Shavit argues that "[t]he Oct. 7 catastrophe fully exposed the enfeeblement" of Israel's strategic thinking. "While the Israeli soldier, the

Israeli civilian, and Israeli society displayed awe-inspiring courage and valor" in the days and weeks following Hamas's slaughter, rape, maiming, and kidnapping, the government "failed to formulate a comprehensive security framework, an effective diplomatic policy, and a convincing international campaign to defend its actions." That remains true notwithstanding Israel's remarkable post–October 7 military achievements, especially of the last few weeks.

A new Israeli national security strategy, maintains Shavit, should be based on the nation's founding doctrines: "Israel must return to the principles of Ze'ev Jabotinsky and David Ben-Gurion—and adapt them to the challenging reality of the twenty-first century." It is necessary but not sufficient for Israel to fortify its iron wall: excel at intelligence gathering and analysis, achieve decisive victories on the enemies' territory, and deter aggression by repeated military successes. In addition, Israel must seize the initiative, placing a priority on acting preemptively not only to prevent Tehran from obtaining nuclear weapons but also to diminish substantially Iran's conventionally armed proxies.

To seize the initiative, argues Shavit, Israel must undertake a variety of tasks. It must reorganize and strengthen the IDF, the Mossad, and the Shabak. It must continually improve cyber and AI capabilities and recommit itself to studying intensively not only its adversaries' military capabilities but also their societies, cultures, political ideologies, and religious beliefs. It must sow division between the terrorists and the civilian populations they exploit. It must punish Iran for its proxies' aggressions. And, crucial to all these improvements and transformations, Israel must undertake large-scale internal political reform: "Israel cannot launch a preemptive war initiative without trustworthy leaders, sound government, a strong army—and a unified society that recognizes itself as engaged in a righteous existential struggle against its adversaries."

This ambitious new security strategy, Shavit emphasizes, will have to contend with "two calamitous scenarios": a resource-depleting and spirit-sapping war of attrition and an all-out regional war. To avert the one and prepare for the other, Israel must expand its defense industries, safeguard its partnership with the United States, draw more moderate Arab and Muslim nations into the Abraham Accords, and openly and emphatically join forces with the rest of the free world in the struggle against the authoritarian powers, foremost among them the Chinese Communist Party, Russia, and Iran.

Shavit advises Israel to postpone a final showdown with Iran for a few years. This would give the Jewish state time to reinforce its iron wall, rebuild its military, and recommit to the mix of Athenian and Spartan virtues that formed it and enabled it to prevail and prosper.

However, Iran's firing of at least 180 ballistic missiles at Israel on October 1—a second major act of war following its mid-April barrage of more than 300 drones, cruise missiles, and ballistic missiles—may throw off Shavit's preferred timetable. Although they had the potential to cause immense loss of life and extensive damage to infrastructure, Iran's ballistic missiles did little harm because Israel's extraordinary air-defense systems—along with the efforts of the United States and Jordan—intercepted nearly all of them. Nevertheless, Israel promises a "harsh response" to Iran's aggression.

Whatever the coming days bring, Israel's "**decade of do-or-die**," according to Shavit, will require the nation to mobilize in multiple spheres.

Military mobilization must include significantly enlarging the armed forces, regular and reserves; expanding ground forces; strengthening offensive and defensive cybercapabilities; reforming leadership ranks; tripling ammunition stores; improving civilian readiness for attacks on the home front; and maximizing strategic independence by becoming "**a global leader in defense production.**"

Civic mobilization undergirds military mobilization. Accordingly, Israel's educational system must "cultivate a new spirit of pioneerism." Minority communities must do their part. The ultra-Orthodox should serve in the Home Front Command. So should young Israeli men and women who have avoided military service, as well as men between the ages of 45 and 65 who have fulfilled their regular and reserve responsibilities. And Arab Israelis—some 21 percent of the population—should contribute to "the nation's defense by serving in hospitals, clinics, the medical corps, firefighting, and other non-military essential services."

Diplomatic mobilization is crucial as well. Israel, argues Shavit, should entrench itself within the world's freedom bloc by devising realistic plans, consistent with Israel's security imperatives, for rebuilding and stabilizing Gaza and improving freedom and social and economic wellbeing among West Bank Palestinians. The Jewish state must tighten security cooperation with the United States, normalize relations with Saudi Arabia, renew partnerships with Europe, and deepen relations with India. It must become a manufacturing powerhouse of sophisticated weapons systems, both to equip its own armed forces, which will make it more self-reliant, and to contribute to the free world's military needs, which will enhance its international stature. It must use its cyber capabilities to stir unrest among the abused populations that live under Hezbollah's and Hamas's theological tyrannies. And it must persuade friends and partners to join in weakening Iran through economic sanctions and the fomenting of internal dissent.

Military mobilization, civic mobilization, and diplomatic mobilization hinge on political mobilization. Afflicted by "cynicism, mediocrity, and truculence," Israel's politicians have weakened the nation's cohesion, asserts Shavit. To fashion a governing coalition and constitutional order worthy of its remarkable people, Israel should hold elections at the first opportunity. While Shavit was composing his book during the first half of 2024, that meant after the northern and southern borders had been stabilized. Iran's massive missile attack last week has changed those calculations. Given Prime Minister Netanyahu's declaration that "[t]he regime in Iran does not understand our determination to defend ourselves and our determination to retaliate against our enemies," there is no saying when a realistic opportunity for new elections will arise.

When Israel can safely hold elections, urges Shavit, the nation's large Zionist majority—right and left—should form a national unity government. If war with Iran still looms, the broad coalition "should establish a narrow emergency cabinet, with a wide mandate to focus on preparing Israel." It should also present a "'thin' constitution," one covering basic government institutions and the separation of powers that can earn wide popular support and secure the Jewish state as a rights-protecting democracy. The national unity government should also make a priority of revitalizing the civil service and incorporating the ultra-Orthodox and Arab minorities into Israeli civic life.

Whether full-scale regional war breaks out in the short term or in the intermediate term, Israel must, over the long term, Shavit concludes, renew its multifaceted founding spirit. The Jewish state must replace the "**divisiveness and grievance**" that plague its political culture with a spirit of "**mutual responsibility**." Israel "must be steadfast and fierce, but it must never be belligerent and wild." The Jewish state must honor the laws of war even as its enemies defy them. It must remain "**an oasis of liberty**" as it battles "authoritarianism and fanaticism." And it must prepare for war to attain peace. By combining rival but essential virtues, maintains Shavit, Israelis "will ensure that the cruel conflict in which we find ourselves does not corrupt us, and does not cause us to lose our way and our souls."

One might take issue with any number of premises, observations, claims, judgments, and proposals that Shavit sets forth in his bold sketch of a new Israeli national security strategy. Such are the stakes, the complexities, and the contingencies that on any particular point, some will decry him for going too far, and others will condemn him for not going far enough. On the essential matter, though, Shavit has made a decisive case: to remain free, democratic, Jewish, and secure in the post–October 7 world, Israel must surpass Athens and Sparta by blending the best in both.